TWAYNE'S WORLD AUTHORS SERIES

A Survey of the World's Literature

SOVIET UNION

Sergey Esenin

TWAS 478

Sergey Esenin

SERGEY ESENIN

By CONSTANTIN V. PONOMAREFF

University of Toronto

TWAYNE PUBLISHERS
A DIVISION OF G. K. HALL & CO., BOSTON

Library of Congress Cataloging in Publication Data

Ponomareff, Constantin V
    Sergey Esenin.

    (Twayne's world authors series; TWAS 478:
    Soviet Union)
    Bibliography: pp. 187–89
    Includes index.
    1. Esenin, Sergey Aleksandrovich, 1895–1925—Criticism and
interpretation.
PG3476.E8Z8494   891.7′1′42   77–20287
ISBN 0–8057–6319–8

To my parents

Contents

About the Author

Constantin V. Ponomareff is an Associate Professor of Russian Literature at the University of Toronto, Scarborough College, and has written in the fields of nineteenth and twentieth century Russian literary criticism, poetry and comparative literature.

Preface

To date no study of the juxtaposition of Esenin's poetic vision and the critical response to it by his contemporaries in the decade after 1917 has appeared in English or, for that matter, anywhere in the West. In contrast to a growing but prescriptive interest in Esenin studies in the Soviet Union, especially in the years after Stalin's death in 1953 (and following a quarter century of near silence before that), little has been written specifically about Esenin in the West. What has appeared stems either from the pens of an older, mainly émigré, generation of poets, writers, critics, and scholars, or from a younger generation of university teachers across Europe and North America.

My original reason for writing this study was a sense of the disparity that I felt existed between Esenin's poetic vision and its critical interpretation by his contemporaries. I could, of course, never be sure of penetrating fully into the world of Esenin's poetic imagination, but I did believe that I could in effect redirect the focus of his contemporary critics.

This involved, above all, a less arbitrary approach to Esenin's poems, a willingness to let them speak for themselves much more freely before imposing an interpretive structure on them. Hence in Part I I have worked at close range with the inner relationships of Esenin's poetic imagery, which is central to his creative vision. Although formalist to a point, this approach has not prevented me from tracing the psychological and social semantics and implications of Esenin's metaphorical language. It is with this in mind that I also introduced the biographical chapters of Part I (Chapters 1, 3, 5), in order to create a further personal and existential context for my analysis of Esenin's creative imagination, the nature of his lyrical energy (Chapters 2, 4, 6, 7). Part II, apart from describing the specifics of contemporary critical response to Esenin's poetic work, also attempts to define the distance separating poetic intent, on the one hand, from its interpretation, on the other.

The range of this study is limited by the year 1927 partly because the criticism discussed satisfies the aims enunciated above, but also because that year is a convenient cutoff point both poetically for Esenin and historically for the 1920s: after 1927 came Esenin's fall into official disrepute and, not coincidentally, an increasing regimentation of Russian culture and life.

There are two further limitations. I have not dealt with Esenin's prose, which is artistically and psychologically weak. Nor have I expanded the study to include Western and post-Stalin criticism. Much of this criticism (especially the Soviet Russian) has been politically motivated, and would merely have increased the range of the study and widened the distance between poetic vision and its interpretation.

A final note: in referring to Esenin's collected works, I have used the five-volume edition of 1961–1962, even though there is a more recent edition of 1966–1968.[1] Citations by volume and page in the text are to this edition.

In closing, I should like to thank my wife Barbara for being the first reader of this book, and for her many understanding ways of keeping the world at bay while it was being written.

CONSTANTIN V. PONOMAREFF

University of Toronto

Chronology

1895   Born October 3, new style, in the village of Konstantinovo, Ryazan province.

1899   Goes with his mother to live with maternal grandparents.

1903–   Begins writing poetry.
1904

1909–   Sent to Spas-Klepiki, a private teachers' seminary; con-
1912   tinues to write poetry and read literature. July: comes to Moscow for a little over six months.

1913   Spring: returns to Moscow in quest of poetic recognition. Autumn: enrolls in evening courses in Russian literature given at A. L. Shanyavsky's Popular University. Joins the Surikov Literary-Musical Circle, for young proletarian and peasant writers.

1914   Spring: marries Anna Izryadnova. Continues his university studies.

1915   January: first son born. Early spring: goes to Petrograd to seek his poetic fortune. March 9: meets Alexander Blok, who helps him publish his work. Exempted from military service on medical grounds. Autumn: meets the peasant poet Nikolay Klyuev, frequents literary salons.

1916–   Publishes first collection of poems *Radunitsa* (*Mourning*
1917   *for the Dead*). Serves on the tsarina's hospital train in Tsarskoe Selo, but the February 1917 revolution finds him in a disciplinary battalion. Avoids military service in the summer of 1917. August 1917: marries Zinaida Raykh. Meets the "Scythian" critic Ivanov-Razumnik, contributes to his journal *Skify* (*The Scythians*).

1918   Publishes collections of poetry: *Goluben'*; *Isus-mladenets* (*The Infant Jesus*); *Preobrazhenie* (*Transfiguration*), *Sel'skii chasoslov* (*Rural Breviary*); and a second, revised edition of *Radunitsa*. In early spring settles in Moscow. May: daughter born. In the autumn meets Anatoly Mariengof.

1919   Helps found the Imaginist movement in the early part
        of the year. Tries unsuccessfully to join the Communist
        Party. Feverish creative activity.

1920   Publishes second, revised edition of *Goluben'*, as well as
        collections *Treriadnitsa* and *Tripitkh* (*Tryptich*). March:
        son born. Travels through Russia and the Caucasus.

1921   Publishes *Ispoved' khuligana* (*Hooligan's Confession*);
        second editions of *Isus-mladenets, Treriadnitsa,* and *Preo-
        brazhenie*; a third edition of *Radunitsa*. Restless, visits
        Turkestan and Tashkent. Meets the famous American
        dancer Isadora Duncan.

1922   Publishes *Izbrannoe* (*Selected Works*) and *Pugachev*;
        also the first volume of a two volume *Sobranie stikhov i
        poem* (*Collected Lyric and Narrative Poetry*). Early
        May: marries Isadora Duncan in Moscow.

1922   May 10–August 23, 1923: Esenin and Duncan visit Ger-
        many, Belgium, France, Italy, and the United States. In
        Berlin Esenin suffers a nervous breakdown. September
        to January spent in the United States. Upon arriving in
        France, Esenin has difficulties with the authorities and
        finally is put into a private mental hospital. Duncan
        returns with Esenin to Russia on August 3: though never
        formally divorced, they separate, and Duncan leaves
        Russia in 1924.

1923   Publishes *Stikhi skandalista* (*Verse of a Creator of Scan-
        dals*). September: marries Galina Benislavskaya. Drinks
        heavily, begins to suffer from delirium tremens, hallucina-
        tions, persecution mania, and suicidal tendencies.

1924   Publishes collections *Moskva kabatskaia* (*Tavern Mos-
        cow*) and *Stikhi* (*Poems, 1920–1924*). January: spends
        time in a sanatorium; March: briefly hospitalized. Grows
        restless over the summer. Lives in the Caucasus from
        early September until February 1925. In December meets
        Shagane Nersesovna Terteryan, the "Shagane" of his
        Persidskie motivy (*Persian Motifs*). Several attempts to
        visit Persia fail.

1925   Publications: poem *Pesn' o velikom pokhode* (*Song of the
        Great Campaign*), and the following collections of poetry:
        Rus' sovetskaia (*Soviet Rus'*); *Strana sovetskaia* (*Land of*

the Soviets); *Berezovyi sitets* (*Birch Chintz*, a new title for his *Izbrannoe* of 1922); *Izbrannye stikhi* (*Selected Poetry*); *O Rossii i revoliutsii* (*On Russia and Revolution*); and *Persidskie motivy*. March-September: moves back and forth between Moscow and the Caucasus. His natural son A. S. Esenin-Volpin is born. September: marries Sofya Tolstaya, a granddaughter of Leo Tolstoy. Works on his poem "Chernyi chelovek" ("The Black Man"). November: enters a Moscow psychiatric clinic but leaves it in late December to start a new life in Leningrad. December 28: hangs himself from the water-pipes in the "icon corner" of his room in the Hotel d'Angleterre, just across from St. Isaac's Cathedral in Leningrad.

CHAPTER 1

From Village to City

I 1895–1912: Konstantinovo and Spas-Klepiki

SERGEY Esenin was born on October 3, 1895, in the village of Konstantinovo, Ryazan province. Relations between Esenin's parents were strained, and so, when Esenin was about four, his mother took him away and went to live with her parents. As Esenin's younger sister Alexandra remembers it, the household was lively and merry, full of of songs and accordian music.[1]

Esenin's maternal grandparents exerted a major influence upon his life. Esenin remembered that on weekends his grandfather sang plaintive ancient songs to him, and told him stories from the Bible and from religious history.[2] His grandmother was a kind and compassionate woman. Devout and pious, she would often take the small boy on pilgrimages to outlying monasteries. Her house was always open to all manner of pilgrims, who repaid her hospitality by singing "spiritual songs" and legends about paradise and popular saints. Esenin later recalled listening to her fairy tales: since he never liked their unhappy endings, he changed them to suit himself. He felt, in retrospect, that it was his grandmother who had motivated him to write poetry. He began writing at the age of eight.[3]

Esenin's relatively happy and carefree childhood, spent in Konstantinovo and the surrounding countryside, must have stimulated his budding poetic sensibility even more.[4] When he was nine he began to attend the local village school. In 1907 he had to repeat his third year because he neglected his studies, but he finished his primary schooling in 1909, and received a testimonial to the great strides he had made in his schoolwork.[5]

The family wanted Esenin to become a rural schoolteacher, and so dispatched him to a private teachers' seminary in the

village of Spas-Klepiki.[6] Evgeny Khitrov, one of Esenin's senior
teachers during his three year stay there, recalled that Esenin
loved church services and the singing of the choir. There were
many aspiring young poets among the pupils there, he tells us,
and it was only the ease with which Esenin handled rhyme and
metre that distinguished him from his classmates. When Esenin
brought him his poem "Zvezdy" ("The Stars," 1911–1912), he
recognized the boy's talent, and suggested to him that the poem
might be published.[7]

Esenin himself has admitted to an unsystematic bent of mind
and a dislike of intellectual discipline. He became so tired of methods and pedagogy at the Spas-Klepiki Seminary that he would
not hear of going on to a pedagogical institute in Moscow.[8]
Though Esenin claims the seminary only gave him a good knowledge of Old Church Slavonic,[9] Khitrov suggests that it was in the
seminary that Esenin first began reading more widely than
was necessary for his schoolwork. And when Esenin had com-
pleted his courses in 1912, it was Khitrov who advised him to
settle either in Moscow or St. Petersburg and to devote himself
to the study of literature under somebody's guidance. He was
gratified to see that Esenin followed his advice.[10]

II 1913–1915: Moscow and Petrograd

When Esenin arrived in Moscow in March of 1913, his search
for poetic acclaim and fame had begun. His dream was to
become a real poet.[11]

In 1914 Esenin married Anna Izryadnova (1891–1946), who
has left us descriptions of Esenin's arrogant, proud, ambitious,
and possessive nature. They had a son in January of 1915, but
by March Esenin was off to Petrograd to seek his literary fortune.
He visited Moscow and Konstantinovo from time to time,
dropping in on his wife on the way to Petrograd.[12]

For a year and a half Esenin had attended evening courses
in Russian literature given by eminent scholars at Moscow's
A. L. Shanyavsky Popular University. Esenin's childhood friend
Nikolay Sardanovsky recalls that Esenin took one of his early
poems to Professor Pavel Sakulin, then lecturing at the university, whose comments flattered the young man.[13]

The poet Ryurik Ivnev (1891–   ), who first met Esenin during the winter of 1914 at a Petrograd poetry reading, remarked on Esenin's tremendous drive for poetic recognition: "Of course he knew his own worth. And his modesty was but a thin cover underneath which beat a greedy, insatiable yearning to conquer everyone with his poems, to subdue and to overpower everybody completely."[14] Esenin soon realized that the literary capital of Russia was Petrograd, not Moscow. The poet Nikolay Livkin (1894–   ), who met Esenin in Moscow in 1915, quoted Esenin as saying: " 'No! One can't get anywhere here in Moscow. I'll have to go to Petrograd. I mean, what can you do! All the letters with my poems are being returned. Nothing of mine is being printed. No, I'll have to do it myself somehow. . . . Water will not flow under a stone. You have to take glory and fame by the horns.' "[15] He added that he would go to Petrograd and see one of the leading Symbolist poets of the time, Alexander Blok, who would understand him.[16]

III *1915–1917: War and Revolution*

In his autobiography of May 1922, Esenin recalled that he broke out in a sweat when he saw Blok, the first real poet he had ever met.[17] At that meeting, on March 9, 1915, Esenin read his poems to Blok. In a letter of recommendation, Blok spoke of Esenin as a "naturally gifted peasant poet" and listed six of his poems that were worth publishing.[18]

A letter that Blok sent to Esenin on April 22, 1915, indicates that Esenin had wanted to see him again to talk about his future. Blok postponed the meeting, but wrote in his letter: "I do think that your path will perhaps not be a short one. In order not to stray from it, you must not hurry or be nervous. For each step that one makes, one will have to answer sooner or later, and to make one's way now is difficult. It is probably most difficult of all in literature."[19] Esenin noted in his 1923 autobiography that the best journals of that time (1915) began to publish his writing. When his first collection of poems *Radunitsa* (*Mourning for the Dead*), appeared in the autumn of 1915 (it was actually published in February 1916), everyone thought him a gifted poet, he said. Characteristically, he added that he knew that better than anyone else.[20] Blok had thus helped gain him entrance into the major literary journals of the time.

Another important figure in Esenin's life was the older peasant poet Nikolay Klyuev, whom he met in the autumn of 1915. The poet and critic Sergey Gorodetsky (1884–1967) has described Klyuev's personal and poetic impact on Esenin and others.[21]

The First World War had been raging for some time, but Esenin did not wish to enlist and instead spent the year 1915 (from the end of April until October) in Konstantinovo writing poetry. Eye trouble had temporarily freed him from the draft.[22] Thanks to influential friends[23]—but no doubt also as a result of the court's desire at that time to attract artists and poets coming from the people, like Klyuev and Esenin[24]—Esenin next found himself on the tsarina's hospital train in Tsarskoe Selo. From April 20, 1916, to February 23, 1917, Esenin served and entertained hospitalized troops. He attended church services in the Imperial Fedorovsky Cathedral, for which even aristocratic notables had to have special passes. Esenin also participated in a concert during which, in the presence of the empress and her daughters, he read his poetry and received a gold watch whose chain came from the tsar's personal possessions.[25] Esenin could hardly have risen higher.

But then Esenin's star began to fall. He himself has supplied one reason for this in his autobiography of 1923, where he says that the February revolution of 1917 found him at the front in a disciplinary battalion because he had refused to write poetry in honor of the tsar.[26] The poet Vadim Shershenevich on the other hand, believed Esenin had been expelled from Tsarskoe Selo for his democratic poem "Marfa Posadnitsa" ("Marfa the Mayoress," 1914).[27]

Whatever the reason, Esenin implicated the socialist-revolutionary sympathizer and "Scythian" critic Ivanov-Razumnik (pseudonym of Razumnik Ivanov) in his refusal to serve the tsar: "I kept refusing, seeking advice and support in Ivanov-Razumnik."[28] He had often met Ivanov-Razumnik during the early stages of his Petrograd stay.[29] In an unpublished speech of 1926, the Marxist critic V. Lvov-Rogachevsky (pseudonym of Vasilii Lvovich Rogachevsky) confirmed the fact that Esenin, while in Tsarskoe Selo, saw Ivanov-Razumnik often.[30]

It is not surprising, then, that Esenin welcomed the February revolution of 1917. Ivnev recalls that for a few days thereafter[31] Esenin was as if drunk, and adds: "He was undoubtedly one of the few poets who were going in step with the revolution."[32] Esenin, by his own admission, deserted from the army and cast his lot with the socialist revolutionaries, not as a party worker, but as a poet.[33] (Esenin's second marriage, to Zinaida Raikh [1894–1939] falls into this period. In his 1924 autobiography, Esenin describes this period in a sentence and a half, saying nothing at all about his first marriage.)[34] He spent the summer and autumn of 1917 in Konstantinovo writing poetry,[35] and began publishing in Ivanov-Razumnik's journal *Skify* (*The Scythians*).

When the time came, Esenin also accepted the October revolution enthusiastically, though from a peasant's vantage point. "During the years of revolution, I was entirely on the side of October," he wrote in 1925. "But I interpreted everything in my own way and manner, with a peasant's bias."[36] Esenin came into his own during this period of revolutionary upheaval, when, according to the poet Petr Oreshin, he was able to overcome his creative dependence on both Klyuev and Blok. Klyuev in particular, according to Oreshin, was not revolutionary enough for Esenin,[37] even though Esenin was quick to recognize his poetic talent.[38]

CHAPTER 2

The Early Poetry, 1910–1915

I In Search of the Poetic Self

E SENIN'S early poetry can be viewed as the product of the first of three periods in which Esenin sought to define his poetic voice and find an individual manner of expression. This period of searching, though it did produce a number of personally representative poems, was on the whole imitative. In form and content his work at this time was largely inspired by the oral and literary modes of Russian folk poetry.

Biblical stories, ancient Russian laments, folk songs and fairy tales, the spiritual songs of pilgrims—all left their mark here. Life's experience only corroborated his poetic apprehension: family life, pilgrimages to monasteries, hearing all sorts of folk-tales and poems, church choirs, a pastoral experience of nature and village life sometimes leading to the discovery of striking poetic images only substantiated the reality of the folklore world.

Esenin's populist bent during his Moscow and Petrograd years, even his antimilitarism, were a direct outcome of his peasant experience. His interest in folk poetry, and especially his admiration for the older peasant poet Nikolay Klyuev, clearly suggests the general direction of his quest. Also, he was drawn to Blok probably because he sensed Blok's populist sympathies coupled with a Symbolist sensibility not so very far removed from his own romantic, "otherworldly" sense of existence nurtured by the Russian folk tradition. Esenin's peasant-oriented acceptance of the revolution of 1917 was likewise in keeping with his character.

The early Esenin is thus very much of a piece. The critic Pavel Sakulin, writing in 1916, was correct in pointing up the spiritual unity of Esenin's religiously tinged, pastoral, and popular poetic perception.[1]

20

II *Prosody*

The rhythmic and metric structure of Esenin's early poetry demonstrates his poetic dependence on both folk sources and Russian Symbolism. The poetic meters he used most frequently then are the trochaic ($-\smile$) and dactylic ($-\smile\smile$), which bring his poetry structurally very close to the epic and folksong traditions. His common use of accentual, or even free, verse links his work to both the Russian epic song and Blok's *dol'nik* and *vers libre*. Iambic meters ($\smile-$) occur less frequently, although Esenin seems to have employed them more readily after 1915. Amphibrachic ($\smile-\smile$) and anapestic ($\smile\smile-$) meters are rare, especially if one remembers that some of his lines that resemble anapests are probably more closely related to the Russian epic song, with its two syllable anacrusis at the beginning and dactylic clausula at the end of the line. In considering Esenin's rhythmic and metric debt to folk poetic prosody, it may be well to add at this point that a metrically intermittent iambic and trochaic cadence is also characteristic of Russian epic poetry; and that Esenin, who knew the poems of Russia's first peasant poet, Aleksey Koltsov (1809–1842), stayed away from the latter's monotonously stylized poetry with its mostly iambic, amphibrachic, and anapestic meters—meters that (apart from the above qualification for the iambic) are essentially foreign to the folk poetic medium.

Esenin's rhyme structure is traditional (masculine, feminine, and dactylic rhymes), but he displays a predilection for assonance. It is here that one may speak of a Symbolist influence, and especially Blok's. But in Esenin's two longer poems—"Pesn' o Evpatii Kolovrate" ("The Song about Evpaty Kolovrat," 1912) and "Marfa the Mayoress" (1914)—the near absence of rhyme (except for occasional grammatical rhyme and assonance) does bring them closer to the "rhymeless" structure of Russian epic poetry.

Esenin depends upon the folk poetic tradition in yet another way, and this is his connection to the Russian folksong. During Esenin's lifetime and later, many critics noted, either with approbation or censure, the autobiographical character of his poetry, and indeed, Esenin was wont to see himself as an Imagist

poet. These elements of lyrical self-revelation through pastoral
poetic images link Esenin to the Russian folksong tradition. The
Russian folk song, especially the so-called *bytovye pesni* (songs
of everyday Russian life) were, it has been pointed out, a
subjective outpouring of grief or joy, and as such were purely
lyrical. Yet, as each individual poet and singer expressed his or
her experience of Russian life, the folk song distilled collective
experience which in Russia gave a sorrowful aspect to its folk
muse. Proximity to the world of nature provided human grief
a means of expression.

III   *Beginnings of Poetic Vision*

The specific content as opposed to the symbolic significance
of Esenin's early poetry once again demonstrates that he drew on
the world of Russian folk experience in his writing.

Esenin's poetry[2] is rich in impressions of nature and village life.
The proximity of man as poet to nature, and especially his mysterious association with her—that anthropomorphic relation between the natural and human worlds—ultimately casts its own
poetic spell over everything.

But in the very beginning, there are—apart from a rustic's
awareness of nature—no clearly discernible lines of perceptive
development. Spring's shared exuberance yields to stylized love
songs, that may then give way to a budding cosmic sense of
wonder, as in "The Stars." Poems such as "Vospominanie"
("Remembrance," 1911–1912) and "Pesnia starika razboinika"
("The Song of the Old Robber," 1911–1912) are undoubtedly
poetic reminiscences of Aleksey Koltsov's poetry. Such sentimentalized self-reflections as those found in "Moia zhizn'" ("My
Life," 1911–1912) on the other hand, recall both Ivan Nikitin's
and Spiridon Drozhzhin's peasant poems. That this latter poem
provides one of the few examples of anapest meter only under-
lines its imitative quality. The elegiac note in most of these
poems, so typical of the Russian folk song, is amplified by
such motifs as the passage of time, the fading of love and
youth, and the onslaught of old age and death.

But Esenin was already beginning to be aware of his peasant
roots. In a poem called "Poet" ("The Poet," 1912), he spoke of

himself as the bard of the Russian soil: "He is a poet, a national poet, / He is a poet of his native soil" (I, 82). The use of the third person here suggests that he had not as yet found himself completely as a poet of the people, but the lines definitely indicated the direction of his poetic thought. And his poem "Kuznets" ("The Smith," 1914), in its forging of future fearlessness and happiness, anticipates his later longer poem "Inoniia" (1918):

> Fly like a playful vision
> Into the distance beyond the clouds.
> There, far off behind the dark cloud,
> Beyond the threshold of gloomy days,
> The sun's mighty brilliance falls
> On the flat fields.
> Fields and pastures drown
> In the day's light blue radiance,
> And happily out of the plough-land
> Ripen the winter fields. (I, 97–98)

Esenin's preoccupation with the well-being of the Russian peasant again emerged in the image of peasant victory over outside enemies as developed in his poem "Egoriy" (the popular form of St. Gregory, 1914). Like the more legendary folk ballad in which Egoriy gained victory over the Tatars in medieval times, Esenin's poem may by analogy have also had the Germans in mind. But more vital to Esenin's poetic perspective were the protective, regenerative aspects of this agrarian nature saint; his popular image as a symbol of fertility, earth power, and the coming of spring; and his function as the patron of livestock and the animal world. The figure of Egoriy reemphasized Esenin's peasant orientation and pointed directly to his vision of a Russian terrestrial peasant paradise as developed in "Inoniia."

In "Egoriy," which may also be viewed as the poetic opposite of the later poem "Volch'ia gibel'" ("Wolf's End," 1922)— perhaps "Egoriy" is a Russian version of the biblical lion and lamb motif—the white wolves have made peace with the Russian peasant. In stanza twelve they virtually merge with the peasant

ethos of the poem as they venture forth with Egoriy to meet
and overcome the enemy invader encircling them. It is symptomatic of Esenin's pastoral poetic sensibility that in this poem
he could, on his first attempt, create strikingly original images
as, for instance, when Egoriy tells the white wolves of the
terror experienced by the wolf cubs and their mothers before
the advancing enemy. Here the human and animal worlds
coalesce:

> All the she-wolves build their lairs
> In the Murom woods.
> Stars have petrified in their eyes
> Because of their cubs' terror.   (I, 100)

The struggle here was between nature, including the peasant,
and a hostile outside world, whether the "black planet"
(*chernaia planida*) of which Esenin spoke is to be understood
as the Germans or, as is more likely, the industrial urban world,
that proverbial "iron guest," symbolized perhaps in the word
"lokhmonida" (locomotive?): "I sense the coming of the
'lokhmonida'— / You will not make out together" (I, 101).

Esenin's poem "Marfa the Mayoress" (1914) was yet another
poetic expression of the vanquishing of an enemy (he had
already utilized a similar theme in his longer poem "The Song
about Evpatiy Kolovrat" of 1912, which dealt with the Mongol
invasion of Ryazan). This time the "antichrist" who sold his
soul to the devil was the Muscovite Russian tsar himself, whose
kingdom was approaching its preordained end. Marfa and
Novgorod, on the other hand, were allied with God, and
represented eventual liberation from oppression. The structure
of the poem—a cross between an epic poem and a "spiritual
song"—points to the popular character of the impending uprising:
"As in olden times the bell will call from the Veche/ And here,
you people, I'll stop my tale" (I, 313). It is not surprising, given
his hostility toward Muscovy, that Esenin should have welcomed
the Russian revolution of 1917, although from a peasant's point
of view (*s krest'ianskim uklonom*—"with peasant bias").

Many of Esenin's poems during this early period took their
inspiration from the store of Russian folk poetry. Nikolay

Nekrasov's poetic tale "Moroz—Krasnyi nos" ("Father Frost") undoubtedly influenced the conception of Esenin's fairy tale poem "Sirotka" ("The Orphan," 1914), where the Cinderella motif, however, transforms sorrow into happiness. In "Chto eto takoe?" ("What is that?", 1914) he poeticized the Russian riddle. His "Uzory" ("Patterns," 1914), with its six foot trochee, is reminiscent of the more authentic Russian *plachi* (laments) with their more direct subjective expression of sorrow and their trochaic lines marked at beginning and end by the characteristic two syllable anacrusis and dactylic clausula respectively. His poem "Us" ("Cossack Us," 1914), also seems to have drawn freely for its structural and poetic inspiration both upon the heroic "robber" ballad and the lament, although the lamentation of the latter took over completely, crowding out the characteristic social protest of the traditional folk ballad.

Esenin's poem "Zaglushila zasukha zasevki" ("The drought has stifled the sowing," 1914), is noteworthy, not only for the concrete detail of village life it contains, but even more for its mixing of religious and pagan elements. Detail drawn from Russian village life is also to be found in the long poem "Rus'" ("Old Russia," 1914), where his lament for war recruits confronts Esenin's love for his native region. He rejoiced at the attraction he felt for the sorrow of the Russian fields. Though joy might be short-lived here, it was only his love for this humble peasant Russia that made life even bearable for him:

> Oh, Old Russia, my meek native home,
> I keep my love only for you
> Merry is your short-lived joy,
> With its loud songs in the spring meadows.   (I, 148)

A similar love for rural Russia permeated his poem "Tebe odnoi pletu venok" ("To you alone I wreathe a garland," 1915): "Oh, Old Russia, quiet corner, / It is you I love, in you that I believe" (I, 167). And in his "Nasha vera ne pogasla" ("Our faith has not dwindled," 1915), he reaffirmed his intention to seek and find a peasant road to paradise: "The religious pilgrim's way / Is not our sole path to paradise" (I, 174), and

Do not seek me in God,
Do not call me to love and live ...
I shall go by that other road
To lay down my rebellious head   (I, 175)

IV Mourning for the Dead

In his first collection of poetry, *Mourning for the Dead,*
published in February 1916 and containing thirty-two poems
written between 1910 and 1915, Esenin sought to express
the essence of his early poetic vision.

The early poems of this collection were stylized love songs,
and read like a "Russian" counterpart to his "Persian" poems
of 1924. Still, the important emotional events of man's life in
these poems occur in nature. But nature's linkage to human
events was increasingly touched and colored by a religious,
otherworldly poetic perception. Nature images were suddenly
transformed into religious symbols: russet haystacks in the
field under the moon's light turned into churches, and the
wood grouse became a bell calling the faithful to an all-night
service (I, 61). It was, however, characteristic of Esenin that
it was not man as human intermediary, but rather nature which
here sanctified human existence. In another poem, even the
intoxication of spring—bringing with it unclear expectations of
the coming of a bride-to-be—hinted at a religious communion
with another world of experience: "Secret tidings gladden /
And shine into my soul" (I, 62). The poem about the religious
knight-errants ("Kaliki," 1910) wandering across Russia in the
service of the People's Christ (*Spas*), was not only composed in
a religious spirit, but also combined religion with popular
traditions by identifying these beggar-knights in the shepherds'
somewhat skeptical minds (cf. the poem's concluding lines)
with the *skomorokhi,* or traveling minstrels, of long ago. The
poetic projection of the poem suggested that Esenin was just
such a popular bard and religious wanderer.

Somewhat in the style of Blok's Symbolist "Stikhi o Prekrasnoi
Dame" ("Poems to the Beautiful Lady," 1901–1902), (but in
a less ethereal and more pronouncedly peasant manner) the
theme—growing gradually stronger—of the bride meeting her
bridegroom to the accompaniment of accordion music was

expressed in the poem "Zaigrai, sygrai, tal'ianochka, malinovy mekha" ("Play, accordion, play your crimson bellows," 1910–1912). But even though the lexical and rhythmic qualities of the poem reflected merely an ordinary boy-meets-girl situation in the village, its imagery raised it above the usual and brought it closer to Blok's more ideal visions. Thus, when Esenin sang of his beloved's blue eyes, they not only belonged to her but transcended her very being to become corn flowers casting their light over the poet's heart and causing it to burn turquoise. A negative parallelism alluded to the natural, nonhuman origins of his beloved: "Not the twilight has woven its patterns into the lake's currents,/ Your embroidered kerchief has flashed from behind a hill's slope" (I, 69).

In his poem "Matushka v Kupal'nitsu po lesu khodila" ("Mother wandered in the forest on the night of Ivan-Kupala," 1912: the reference is to the feast of St. John the Baptist, June 24), the quasi-religious motif of a mother's giving birth to a child shifted even more in the direction of nature and became, as it were, "paganized." The child, the future poet, was born in the midst of nature on the night of Ivan-Kupala, a time associated in the popular mind with superstition and magic, when nature provides therapeutic herbs, when witches gather on Kiev Mountain, when numerous supernatural forces and creatures are temporarily released, when a tree-fern that blooms at midnight can reveal hidden treasure.

Esenin's poetic birth occurred on that night. Magic grasses pricked his mother's feet before she gave birth to this "grandson of Kupala." He was born amid songs, with the grass for a blanket, and the evening twilight wrapped him in the rainbow (I, 84). The magical twilight of spring forecast happiness for him, though he could not rid himself of forebodings of future adversity.

In the longer poem "Mikola" (the popular name of Saint Nicholas, 1913–1914), the three essential elements of the collection—nature, religion, and the peasant people—were combined into one. The popular saint Mikola became a saint-errant and savior, that "ancient servant of the gods" wandering through rural Russia, past monasteries and taverns, on his way to God's and Christ's paradise. Bringing with him peace and healing

powers, Mikola tried to relieve the suffering and poverty of the
Russian peasants as God had ordered him to do. Like Egoriy, he
also saw to the animals caught by the coming of winter; and it
was in his honor that ploughmen sowed rye in the snow to
prepare the ground for the coming of spring, for rebirth and
life after death.

Especially if we have read the later poem "Inoniya," it is not
difficult to see that in this poem Esenin already fancied himself
a poet in a religious guise, a prophet. Nor is the link between
poet and saint absent here. The pagan, magical healing potency
acquired on St. John's Eve was simply lent to a saint; after all
Esenin moved easily between the natural and the divine. Poetic
potency was thus transformed into the religious power to heal
stricken peasant Russia and prepare it for spiritual rebirth, for a
new life with the coming of spring. Furthermore, the bridal
motif present in the poem linked Mikola to the Esenin of
previous poems: for, as Mikola bathed in the white, foamy water
of a lake and dried himself on birchbark, the birch was termed
a bride, and the whole of surrounding nature assumed a bridal
aspect: "The fir and birch grove/ Has drawn a bridal circle
round itself" (I, 90). The groom was drawing ever closer to
his bride, to the realization of his ideal vision. The femininity
of nature was also hinted at in the image of stars hanging in
the apple trees like the giant braids of sorceresses: "Stars hang
in the apple trees/ Like sorceresses' braids" (I, 92).

It should be noted that the bridal symbolism of this poem
was associated with the journey to paradise. In "Zashumeli nad
zatonom trostniki" ("Reeds have started rustling over the backwater," 1914), the bride was metamorphosed into a maiden-
princess (devushka-tsarevna) weeping by the river. It seemed
that she would be unable to marry come spring because the
wood spirit had frightened her with signs of ill omen. It is
noteworthy—and consistent with Esenin's bridal imagery—that
the bark on a birch in this poem has been gnawed away (I, 117).
Nature's wisps of incense and howling winds take on funereal
connotations. Other poems of 1914 reflected a similar mood, for
example, "Troitsyno utro, utrennii kanon" ("It is the morning of
the Trinity, morning Liturgy"). The funereal feeling was so
strong, in fact, that in "Krai lyubimyi! Serdtsu sniatsia" ("Beloved

region! My heart dreams," 1914) the poet was as close to suicide as his maiden-princess had been. In the first stanza of this poem he dreamed of sunlight filtering into the deep bosom of the waters perceiving the light as haystacks of pure sun, and added: "I should like to lose myself/ in your centichime [*stozvonnykh*] verdure" (I, 119). It is probable that such beautiful but depressing imagery reflected the impact of the war which distorted Esenin's lyrical vision. Yet—just as with Blok's tidal relationship to his beautiful lady—Esenin rallied his forces in order to continue to pursue his vision: "Thoughts with a gentle secret for someone/ I have concealed in my soul" (I, 119).

The bridal motif was further developed in the poem "Poidu v skuf'e smirennym inokom" ("My cap on, I shall go forth a humble monk," 1914), where Esenin in a monk's habit imagined himself wandering to a place symbolizing a world of plenty, a place where "birches' milk/ Flows through the plains" (I, 120). The image of birch milk might suggest that the bride had finally conceived. But since the image was but an imaginative projection in time, the poem only expressed poetic intent, and the poet would reach the imagined realm only in the future. Like Mikola, he passed through villages and prayed at haystacks (again an image of future plenty, of satisfying hunger with bread and yearning with spiritual food). The poet's will to believe in an inevitable peasant utopia—"I want to . . ./ Believe also in the happiness of my fellow man/ In the furrow which resounds with the rye's rustling" (I, 120)—thus continued to mold his vision.

The presence of the divine in human form also in a way symbolically suggested that paradise was close at hand, that the gulf separating it from earthly existence was not unbridgeable. Thus, in "Shel gospod' pytat' liudei v liubovi" ("God went forth to test the people's love," 1914), God wanders across Russia in beggar's guise and finds the peasant people still worthy, since they have not yet lost their capacity for human compassion (I, 122). In "Ne vetry osypaiut pushchi" ("It is not the winds that strip the forest thickets," 1914), the Mother of God herself brought the infant Christ to be sacrificed anew, and left him to walk the Russian earth as a beggar. To the poet, any beggar might be Christ incarnate, and he feared that in the

hour of mysterious revelation (*v tainyi chas*) he would fail to
recognize the presence of the divine: "Archangel's wings in the
fir trees,/ A hungry Savior under a tree stump" (I, 124).

Poems such as "V khate" ("In the peasant hut," 1914), with
its concrete description of peasant life, and "Po selu tropinkoi
krivenkoi" ("Through the village on crooked-drunken paths,"
1914), where peasant recruits were seen off to war, reemphasized
the peasant orientation of Esenin's early work. But he always saw
village life under a godly, transcendental aegis. Thus he portrayed
the peasant hut, whose contents he had just realistically enumer-
ated, two poems further along in the image of the icon: "Hey,
native Old Russia mine,/ The peasant huts look like icons in
their casings" (I, 129). There was no question, however, that
Esenin envisioned his peasant utopia as a paradise on earth,
not in heaven. As the last stanza of the poem has it:

> Should the holy legions cry out to me:
> "Abandon your Old Russia, live in paradise!"
> I'll say: "I don't need paradise
> Give me my native countryside." (I, 130)

These lines echoed his "The religious pilgrim's way / Is not our
sole path to paradise," and yet the spiritual path to his earthly
paradise passed through nature to God, and its prophet Esenin
could not do without either: "I pray to the pale red twilight, /
Receive communion from the brook" (I, 132).

Only through nature's sacrament, through religious communion, could the paradisal vision remain pure until it could
be realized. Hence, in the collection's title poem, "Chuiu
radunitsu bozh'iu–" ("I feel the coming of the divine mourning for the dead," 1914), the three main poetic motifs coalesce
into one: the reality of otherworldly existence—"From birth I
believed / In the resurrection of the Mother of God" (I, 135);
a pantheistic view of nature—"Among pines and fir trees, /
Amid birches' leafy beads, / Under a round wreath of needles, /
I seem dimly to recognize Jesus" (I, 134); nature as God's
inner sanctum—"He [Jesus] calls me into the forest groves, /
As into the Kingdom of Heaven" (I, 134); and the road to
paradise symbolized in Christ's or God's "spirit of the dove,"

that is, the idea of the remission of sins and of regaining paradise lost by dint of hard agricultural labor. All this motivated
the poet's life: "I feel the coming of God's day of the mourning for the dead— / I am not living in vain" (I, 134). And he
exclaimed:

> God's spirit of the dove,
> Like a fiery tongue,
> Has taken possession of my road
> Has stifled my weak outcry.
> The flame pours into the depth of vision.   (I, 134–35)

Analogously, the resurrection of the Mother of God (I, 135)
also suggested the resurrection of one's peasant ancestors, the
occasion for the symbolic celebration of *Radunitsa* in the first
place. Esenin's *Mourning for the Dead* was therefore an affirmative religious projection in time: he sang of life, not death.

Although we may discover the first few hints of his future
religious blasphemy in the poem "Po doroge idut bogomolki"
("Pilgrims on the road," 1914), where the village reacted to
the passage of the religious women pilgrims as if they were
thieves (I, 136), the note was submerged in a series of poems
describing the cheerless isolation of that Russian countryside
that Esenin loved with all his heart: "Krai ty moi zabroshennyi"
("Oh, my desolate region," 1914); "Chernaia, potom propa-
khshaia vyt'" ("Black tract of land, soaked in sweat," 1914);
"Topi da bolota" ("Marshes and swamps," 1914); "Storona,
l' moia, storonka" ("You're my native region," 1915).

In "Ia strannik ubogii" ("I am a poor wanderer," 1915), poet
and nature could still bridge the gulf separating the peasant
from his God and thus ensure an eventual redemption on earth:
"A swallow-tail of the steppe / I sing of God," and "The rapids
sing / Of paradise and spring" (I, 161). But as Esenin's bridal
motif indicates, the original virgin vision had become sullied.
Hence the leitmotif of the sorrowing maiden-princess in "Zashumeli nad zatonom trostniki" ("Reeds have started rustling over
the backwater") was amplified in his poem "Devichnik" ("Pre-
Marriage Party," 1915): "My betrothed will carry me across
the threshold, / He will ask about my maiden honor. / Oh,

friends, I feel ashamed and awkward" (I, 158). His bride's loss
of innocence was illustrated further in the poem "Belaia svitka
i alyi kushak" ("White overcoat and scarlet waist-belt," 1915),
where this time she loved another and would have nothing to
do with the poet: "She splashed laughter in my face" (I, 172).
Secret shame and guilt had been transformed into a provoking
and open rejection of her suitor. In "Tucha kruzhevo v roshche
sviazala" ("The cloud has knitted lace in the grove," 1915),
the poet gave voice to this emotional depression in imagery
suggesting that the road to paradise had become difficult:

> I am driving on a dirty road from the railway station
> Far from my native glades. . . .
> Oh, you've turned cheerless, my native region.   (I, 176)

The last poem of the collection, "Na pletniakh visiat baranki"
("On the wattle fence hang circles of baked dough," 1915),
developed this thought. His vision was not clear: "The sun's
planed shingles / Block out the blue" (I, 177). The time was
dangerous: "Watch yourself, if you're not skilful: / The whirl-
wind will sweep you away like so much dust" (I, 177). Two
lines, borrowing from a well-known Russian gypsy love song
and echoing an earlier image (i.e., "Your embroidered kerchief
has flashed from behind a hill's slope") tried to heal the break in
the "love" theme: "Is it not your shawl with the edging / Which
grows green in the wind?" (I, 177). But the bridal vision (paradise) had suffered a temporary setback:

> Sing of how Stenka Razin
> Drowned his princess.
>
> Is it you, Old Russia, who has scattered
> Your scarlet dress on the road?
>
> Do not judge with severe prayer
> The gaze that has fed on the heart.   (I, 178)[3]

Perhaps Russia would forgive him for now.
   Esenin's early poetry shows him in search of a poetic self. His
peasant orientation is reflected not only formally, in his utiliza-

tion of folk poetics and imagery, but also thematically, in his poetically sustained vision of a future Russian peasant utopia on earth. The imagery of his early poetry is sufficiently consistent to illustrate the gradual development of his dream, although at the end of *Mourning for the Dead* the vision undergoes a certain poetic deformation, for which his biography and the stresses of the social conditions of the time probably bear no small responsibility.

The clearly discernible vision of a future peasant paradise was welded together out of four basic motifs: God, nature, peasant life, and utopia. If Esenin's vision was ultimately this-worldly, its spiritual motivation originated in God and, passing through nature, centered his particular blend of poetic intuition. In this sense, Esenin was, apart from his peasant Imagist poetics, essentially a Romantic. In this sense too, Esenin was poetically quite correct in his autobiographical statement of October 1925, when he observed that it was impossible for him to reject his prerevolutionary *religious* motivation without doing violence to the organic development of his poetic imagination: "I would with pleasure disown many of my religious shorter and longer poems, but they have a great significance for my poetic path before the revolution."[4] To have rejected his religious inspiration would have been tantamount to disowning his peasant poetic focus. That he was not willing to do this (even in 1925) suggests not merely that his religiousness was of a non-Christian, pagan-pastoral character, but also goes far to explain his outbursts of "revolutionary" religious iconoclasm.

CHAPTER 3

The Stall of Pegasus

ESENIN left Petrograd for Moscow in March 1918, along with the Soviet governmental agencies.[1] Petr Oreshin has described how he and Esenin settled in Moscow in the spring of 1918. It was a happy time for Esenin, he remarks: everyone knew of him, he worked hard, and his poems were being published. He had made a name for himself.[2]

It was at a poetry evening at the Moscow Polytechnical Museum in late 1918 that Esenin met the poets Anatoly Mariengof, Vadim Shershenevich, and Ryurik Ivnev, the men who eventually inaugurated the Russian Imaginist movement. In 1923 Esenin spoke of that beginning as follows: "The need which had gathered momentum of carrying into life the power of the image made us realize the necessity for publishing the Imaginist manifesto. We were the creators of a new perspective in the domain of art and we have had to fight a long time."[3] Esenin admitted that he considered the year 1919 the best time of his life.[4]

This may strike us at first as quite surprising, since those were difficult days. The Russian civil war was still raging in the country. Living conditions were very poor, even in Moscow. But according to Ivnev, Esenin was in a privileged position. He had a bookshop, an Imaginist publishing concern, and money; he ate well and dressed well. He was preoccupied with his own literary affairs and plans. For him this was a time of intense poetic creativity. Since the Soviets had banned private enterprise, Esenin's bookshop was one of the very few that could sell books without any official government "orders." The Imaginists worked hard and were able to print many books. For Esenin, this was one of his most productive periods—he would finish a piece of poetry and then publish it.[5]

The reminiscences of Ivan Startsev focus mainly on the

34

Imaginists' bohemian café "The Stall of Pegasus" (*Stoilo Pegasa*), which opened in 1919 and of which he became the manager in 1921. Startsev felt that the notorious "Stall" affected both Esenin's personality and his poetic creativity. Known officially as "The Club of the Association of Freethinkers," it was, says Startsev, a place where bohemians and libertines could meet, in gatherings that usually lasted into the early hours of the morning. There were discussions on art, film, and the theater, as well as poetry readings. Esenin, as chairman of the association, and as almost sole owner of the café, played the main role. He was also one of the best poets of the group. Whenever he read his poetry, the café was filled to overcrowding with an entraptured audience.

Startsev commented that, where art was concerned, Esenin looked at Imaginism from the point of view of his own creative experience. He was indifferent to other forms or types of art. He treated his artistic contemporaries ambivalently, praising them to their faces, but reviling them behind their backs. He became offended when his own poetry failed to please, and some who criticized his poetry became his enemies. His poem "Pugachev," for instance, gave him his greatest statisfaction, and he was embittered when the critics failed to recognize its poetic significance. As for the nature of art, he considered inspired poetic intuition the basis of the creative process, rejecting training or learnedness (*výuchennost'*) in the poet, whose only role, he felt, was to organize his verbal material.[6]

The poet Nikolay Poletaev (1889–1935) has left us a rather unflattering picture of the Esenin of the Imaginist period. Poletaev emphasizes Esenin's envy-ridden, competitive poetic nature. In Poletaev's eyes, Esenin was a scandal-monger who regarded everyone as a "pedestal for his future fame." He would, as a rule, get arrested twice a week. Scandals were a device to attract attention to himself. In his eyes fame was everything, and obscurity synonymous with insignificance. Reputation was the measure of personal dignity. The choice was ultimately fame or death.[7]

In one of his memoirs on Esenin, Georgy Ustinov (1888–1932), who in 1919 was chief editor of the Communist newspaper *Pravda*, wrote of Esenin's unsuccessful attempt to join the

Communist party. The episode reveals yet another aspect of Esenin's drive for poetic acceptance:

Before writing his poem "Nebesnyi barabanshchik" ["The Heavenly Drummer," 1918], Esenin had several times spoken of the fact that he wanted to join the Communist Party. He had even written an application which I had lying on my desk for several weeks. I realized that Esenin, what with all his rough individuality which was alien to any and all discipline, would never make a party man.[8]

Imaginism became Esenin's vehicle for the realization of his poetic dreams and personal ambitions. The proletarian poet Vladimir Kirillov (1890–1943) has sketched a vivid picture of the Imaginist impact on Esenin:

At the time Imaginism began to blossom forth as a sufficiently exuberant hothouse flower. Tens of poets and poetesses were carried away by this fashionable trend. Esenin, with the look of a young prophet about him, tried passionately, full of inspiration, to prove to me the immutability and everlastingness of the theoretical foundations of Imaginism.
"Just realize what a great thing I-magi-nism is! Words have become used up, like old coins, they have lost their primordial poetic power. We cannot create new words. Neologism and transsense language are nonsense. But we have found a means to revive dead words, expressing them in dazzling poetic images. This is what we Imaginists have created. We are the inventors of the new. If you won't go along with us—it's curtains for you, there's nowhere else to go."[9]

It is true, of course, that in time Esenin moved away from Mariengof and Imaginism. Esenin has blamed differences of creative approach as the main cause of the friction between him and other Imaginists.[10] The Imaginist Matvey Royzman (1896–   ) has shed some light on the machinations within the Imaginist group at the time. In his still unpublished reminiscences of Esenin, he remarked that the latter had a "colossal influence" (Royzman's quotation marks) on the Imaginists. Many questions or problems were solved his way, simply because he would stubbornly insist on his way. There were two wings within the Imaginist group. One was headed by Esenin, who considered the image a means of expression and demanded that there be an organic, psychological unity or connection between the images of a poem. The other wing, to which Mariengof belonged, regarded the image as an end in itself and assumed that any connection between images was merely of a technical nature.[11]

In a letter that Esenin sent to Ivanov-Razumnik from Tashkent in early May of 1921,[12] he spoke of the extent of his creative labors during these years. Speaking both patronizingly and critically of Klyuev's and Blok's poetic work, he observed with presumption (and in ungrammatical Russian[13]) that neither Pushkin or Esenin's contemporaries, including himself, knew how to write poetry; but concluded by boasting that he had come to know the nature of art well, had broken it in (*oblomal*), and could for that reason calmly and joyously call himself and his friends "Imaginists."[14]

Poetry and poetic self-aggrandizement were the two forces driving Esenin. In fact, the literary critic Ivan Rozanov (1874–1959) maintained that Esenin feared he might outlive his fame. He was forever bent on poetic self-inflation. In his love of country, for instance, he regarded himself as greater than Blok. In reflecting life truly, he thought himself superior to Klyuev. The Futurist poet Vladimir Mayakovsky, in his eyes, lacked a feeling for the world. So, ultimately, did the Imaginists. Esenin began to dream of comparing himself to Pushkin. Consequently, as an Imaginist, and in his desire to become an all-Russian poet, he began to avoid the use of regional peasant language. Esenin felt a certain anxiety about the inconstancy of fame. Once in 1921 he said to Rozanov: "Generally speaking, a lyrical poet should not live long."[15]

It is not hard to see that Esenin's poetic bias and aggressiveness were isolating him from his gifted literary contemporaries. His overemphasis on the poetic must have separated him still further from life in general. Rozanov has blamed this state of mind and attitude for the emptiness of Esenin's last years, the period that produced his poem "Chernyi chelovek" ("The Black Man").[16] Kirillov, thinking of Esenin's Imaginist period, recalled that Esenin did not need any friends at the time because of his poetic successes.[17] What is more, Esenin was himself aware of

his alienation as a lyrical poet from the temper of the revolutionary times. His fellow poet and friend Semyon Fomin (1881–
1958) remembered a dinner with Esenin in "The Stall of
Pegasus" sometime in 1919. Looking over some of Fomin's poems,
Esenin said: " 'Yes! Our lyrical poetry is good.' He emphasized
the word 'our,' having in mind lyrical poetry in general. 'Only
it isn't in season now. One has to fire with cannons, do you understand, *with cannons!* During such a hurricane they won't hear
this at all.' "[18] In August 1920, Esenin wrote a very revealing
letter to a woman friend. He spoke of how bored and lonely
he was, how confined he felt on the planet earth. Surely there
must be something aside from suicide, he wrote, that would
help him overcome his sense of earthly duality and discord.[19]
Relating an incident that went into the making of his poem
"Sorokoust" ("Prayer for the Dead," 1920)—the attempt by a
young foal somewhere between Tikhoretsk and Pyatigorsk to
outrun the train he was on—Esenin confessed:

Thinking of this incident, I am moved only by grief over the passing
of what is dear, native, and primevally savage (*zverinoe*), and by
the implacable power of the dead and mechanical.
. . . .
. . . I am very saddened now by the fact that history is going
through a difficult epoch in which living individuality is being put
to death. For the socialism on the rise is not at all like the one that
I imagined, but a definite and deliberate one, like some island of
Helena without the glory and without the dreams. The man who
is alive and who is building a bridge to an invisible world finds
himself hemmed in by this socialism; for these bridges are being
cut down and blown up from under the feet of the coming generations. Of course, he whose eyes are opened will then see these
bridges already covered with mould. But it is still always a pity when
a house is built and no one lives in it, and when a canoe is hollowed
out and no one uses it.[20]

CHAPTER 4

The Imagist Period

I *The Road to Paradise*

E SENIN had always considered himself an Imagist poet, even
before his association with the "Imaginists" in early 1919
(see Part II, Chapter 9). His poem "Song about a Dog" (1915),[1]
one of his first more mature and powerful Imagist poems, may
be taken as inaugurating his second creative period, which broke
off temporarily in the spring of 1922 when Esenin suddenly
decided to go abroad.

The creative intensity with which Esenin worked, especially
between 1918 and 1922, the personal poetic ambition and self-
assertion through which he sought poetic recognition and self-
assurance constituted an all-out attempt to establish himself as
a poet. In this emotional venture he did not lose sight of his
original beginnings: he continued to develop his poetic sensibility inspired by nature and folk tradition, and tried to shape
and energize his vision of a future peasant utopia. For a moment
he even thought the revolutionary political upheaval of 1917
corroborated his poetic intuition, and that the renewed spiritual
and existential power of the poetic image could be made to
serve his peasant social dreams. In the years between 1918 and
1922, this romantic vision reached its culminating and breaking
point.

II *"Song about a Dog" and the Development of Poetic Theme*

Essenin's "Pesn' o sobake" ("Song about a Dog") and its poetic
impact demonstrated that Esenin was achieving greater poetic
independence. The poem deals with the fate of a mother-bitch
who loses her seven pups to her "sullen owner," but in merging

39

the human and animal worlds, Esenin somehow managed to instill into his poem a sense of personal poetic destiny. There was something prophetic of the ultimate failure of his vision, therefore, in the poem's concluding lines, where the bitch's eyes "rolled into the snow / like golden stars" (I, 188) as she wept for her pups in the night.

The vision of a bright peasant future had not left Esenin; and, as in his early period, nature still bore the religious and erotic symbolism of future promises: "I sing poetry about serene paradise"; "I get caught by the sticky earrings of birches / Whose foliage reaches to the ground" (I, 189); or,

> With careful step the wind dressed as monk
> Tramples on leaves at the roadsides
> And kisses the invisible Christ's red wounds
> On the rowan-berry bush. (I, 193)

The following lines, for example, continued the bridal motif:

> In a foam of roses the morning dawn turns misty,
> Like the depths in the eyes of a bride.
> Spring has come, like a pilgrim woman from far away,
> With her walking staff and bast shoes of birch bark
>
> In the shady grove she has hung
> the cheerful earrings on the birches.   (I, 195)

A number of poems reverted to the ominous imagery of his early period:

> Fires burn beyond the river,
> Moss and stumps are burning.
> Oh, *kupalo*, oh, *kupalo*,
> Moss and stumps are burning.
>
> The wood-spirit weeps near a pine—
> He pities last year's spring   (I, 197)

But a poem such as "Molot'ba" ("The Threshing," 1915–1916) quickly recaptured the promise: "The dry wheat spike is fertile— / The homemade brew will be heady" (I, 199).

Nonetheless, Esenin sometimes had misgivings about the realization of his vision, for example, in the beautiful but suicidal poem "Ustal ia zhit' v rodnom kraiu" ("I am tired of living in my native region," 1915–1916), where he envisaged being driven from the threshold by his beloved, she "whose name I treasure" (I, 200). And amid his poetic yearning—"You [native countryside] yearn for rose-colored heavens / And for clouds that are of the spirit of the dove" (I, 203)—there were such powerfully evocative poems as "Ne brodit', ne miat' v kustakh bagrianykh" ("No more wandering for me, no more trampling in the purple bushes," 1915–1916), where he gave full expression to his poetic and social forebodings:

> With your sheaf of oaten hair
> You will nevermore pass through my dreams.
> . . . .
> Only in the folds of your crumpled shawl there remains
> The honeyed fragrance of innocent hands.
> . . . .
> Even if from time to time blue evening whispers
> That you were a song and dream.
> Still, whoever made your supple waist and shoulders
> Has with lips at sacred sources been.   (I, 204–205)

In this apotheosis of his poetic creativity, Esenin expressed the thought that nothing could destroy the memory of his beloved, here likened to poetic vision, to a song and a dream. And even if she were never to pass again through his dreams, the one who had created her had drawn from a sacred source.

III   *The Poems of 1916–1918*

Esenin was in fact torn by doubt at this time as to the viability of his poetic and social vision of a peasant utopia. His "bridal" imagery in particular suggested this dilemma. Thus a sensual vision of a young, almost mythical, girl (*lada*) bathing in a lake, her firm breasts reminding the poet of succulent pears (I, 209), could suddenly yield to an image of spiritual bankruptcy and disenchantment, as in "Nishchii s paperti" ("Church beggar," 1916), where a crippled beggar and an old woman represented the utter disintegration of that erotic youthful vision:

Eyes like faded burdock,
. . . .
Once upon a time he was a good shepherd,
. . . .
And here's the old woman in the corner,
. . . .
She was his love
And his intoxicated dream in the green borderland. (I, 210)

Sometimes he felt as though orphaned in his own land (I, 217),
his heart an "afflicted corner" (bol'noi ugolok, I, 219). Only Old
Russia (Rus') provided him some sense of balance:

Oh, Old Russia,—raspberry-colored field that you are,
And the blue that has fallen into the river—
With a joy that ranges on pain
I love your lakelike melancholy. (I, 220)

and

I will not give away these chains,
And I shall not part with my long-lasting dream,
When my native steppes resound
With the prayers carried by the feather grass. (I, 221)

Many lines speak of the conflict between the real and the
ideal within Esenin: "The eyes that have seen the earth, / Are
in love with another earth" (I, 223). This opposition between the
earthly matter of rustic existence and the visionary ideal was
well expressed in his poem "Goluben'" (1916), a title that was
a neologistic substantivization of the "spirit of the dove." Here
his images acquired greater palpability, nature became even more
personified, and poetic thought so highly compressed that two
lines alone could convey both the poet's spiritual conflict and
his vision: "Dusk dances amid an alarmed swarm of jackdaws /
Having bent the moon into a shepherd's horn" (I, 225).

Occasionally he felt as if he were in "mute captivity" (I, 227),
only to burst forth once more in unforgettable lines of poetry:
alienated from himself and others, he had somewhere in an open
field borderland (u mezhi) torn his shadow from his body,
and the shadow left him, taking with it only his bent shoulders:

> With every day I become a stranger
> To myself and to those life brings me close to.
> Somewhere in a clear field, at the borderland,
> I tore my shadow from my body.
>
> She went away naked,
> Taking my stooped shoulders.
> She is probably somewhere further off now,
> Gently embracing somebody else. (I, 227)

Since the Russian word for "shadow" is feminine, in the second stanza Esenin could play on the bridal motif and his "sexual" abandonment.

Even nature turned pensive: "The road lies pensive waiting for its evening, / The rowanberry bushes are murkier than any depth" (I, 235), he wrote, continuing the imagery of an earlier poem where, thinking of paradise, he had spoken of a pilgrim wind kissing the rowanberries as if they were actually Christ's wounds (I, 193). Esenin still displayed a remarkable sense of idealistic determination:

> And along the plains we will come
> To the truth that lies in the peasant's cross,
> To feed on the light
> Of the book of the dove. (I, 241)

In his poem "Pokrasnela riabina" ("The rowanberries have turned redder" I, 243–44), he simply proclaimed that the Christ (*Spas*) had already appeared and brought healing to his native region (I, 243). Esenin employed even more explicitly religious terminology, cast in rustic guise, in announcing the coming of his envisioned utopia, his "new Nazareth" and the cosmic birth of a new God by a ewe. This poem, "Tuchi s ozhereba" ("The clouds from the place where mares give birth," I, 249), was one of the first poetic forerunners of "Inoniia."

In retrospect, the year 1916 seems a year of emotional conflict. Both doubt as to his social vision and uncertainty about himself as a poet assailed him. No poem brings this inner discord out more clearly than his "Propliasal, proplakal dozhd' vesennii" ("Spring rain has finished dancing, weeping" I, 254–55), where

he used the biblical "My God, My God, wherefore hast thou
forsaken me?" to express his feelings and his quandary
about the power of poetry to bring about spiritual and social
transformation:

> Boring to listen to the rush of invisible wings
>   Under the heavenly tree:
> You will not wake ancestral graves
>   With your singing!
>
> The distance of your times has been made earthbound
>   By the word.
> Your dream, I guess, will not resound in the winds,
>   But in heavy tomes.
>
> Someone will sit down, arch his shoulders,
>   Unbend his fingers.
> Your promised evening is close to being realized for someone,
>   But you are not needed.
>
> The promised evening will rouse Bryusov and Blok,
>   Will stir up others.
> But just as always the day will rise from the east,
>   And the moments flare.
>
> Your singing will not change the face of the earth
>   And it will not cause one leaf to fall . . .
> Forever your red lips touched by poetry
>   Are nailed to the tree.

Esenin, furthermore, made an important distinction between
poetry as a literary phenomenon, and as an existential one. In
the former case, no matter how important from the point of
view of literary history, poetry was simply worthless in human
terms if it could not change the face of the earth or touch nature
itself. This was one of the first poetic indications that Esenin
would certainly dedicate himself to something (e.g., the revolution, or the Imaginist movement) that promised a "revolutionary" existential function for the poet's craft. Hence too,
when the revolution came—and it was only steps away—it could
not help infusing new life both into his conception of the

aesthetic function of poetry and its use in his social "paradisal" imaginings.

This is why, if Esenin seemed beset by doubts in 1916, the poems of 1917 up to the October revolution spoke with increasing confidence that, finally, the day of earthly transfiguration was at hand. Nature whispered the secret (I, 257); a mother swan sacrificed her life to an eagle in order that her swan children might escape (I, 261); an icon of the Mother and Child announced the bright joy (I, 262). All the longer poems of 1917 (perhaps with the qualified exception of "Tovarishch" ["The Comrade"], whose proletarian motif intruded artificially into Esenin's rustic theme) spoke of an impending peasant victory. In "Pevushchii zov" ("Otherworldly Call") we find the lines: "The flame is just born / In a peasant manger" (I, 268); in "Otchar'" the lines: "Hail to you Otchar', / Rejuvenated peasant" (I, 273); and "The twilight is like a she-wolf ... / And the animal senses / ... / Jeweled portals / And a star-covered rebirth" (I, 275); and "Oh, today is spring" (I, 276). The poet asks his peasant hero Otchar' to hurl the earth into the heavens and exclaims:

> . . . .
> There sheaves of moon bread
> Gleam golden.
>
> . . . .
> There hunger and thirst
> Do not sing at their roots,
>
> . . . .
> There decrepit time
> Wandering in the meadows,
> Calls all the Russian tribes
> To the feast.   (I, 276–77)

In another poem Esenin rejoiced: "The snows have fed the earth with joy, / Ancient grandfather dreams of Jordan's shores" (I, 278). He perceived his native region (*rodina*) in the image of a cow, in the poem "Oktoikh" ("Church Octet for Voice"): "There is nothing better or more beautiful / Than your bovine eyes" (I, 280). The imagery of this poem, with its visualization of resurrection, purification, and liberation, anticipates "Inoniia":

> Oh God,
> Is it you
> Rocking the earth in its dreams?
> The dust of constellations
> Sparkles in our hair.   (I, 282)

And also: "The hills sing of paradise. / And in that paradise I see / You, my native region" (I, 283).

The very next poem recorded a vision of paradisal plenty in return for peasant sufferings:

> Whether I look into the field or into the heavens,
> I see paradise in both.
> Once again my unploughed native region
> Drowns in shocks of grain.
>
> Once again there are herds without number
> In unshepherded groves,
> And golden streams of water
> Flow down the green hills.
>
> Oh, I believe that for all the torments experienced
> Somebody pours out his gentle arms
> Milk-white
> Over the ruined peasant.   (I, 285)

His vision was renewed, his eyes had recovered their lost power: "Somebody mysterious has fed my eyes / With a serene light" (I, 286). Some images were suggestive of ripeness, as in "On the branch of a cloud, like a plum, / A ripe star sparkles in gold" (I, 288). A new Russia was rising on the horizon.

> Oh, Russia, try your wings,
> Raise another inaccessible fortress!
> A new steppe with new names
> Arises.   (I, 290)

The peasant poets Koltsov and Klyuev, as well as he, had long been on the road to paradise, and Esenin challenged the old heavens:

> But secretly I continue my dispute
> Even with God's mysteries.
>
> I knock the moon down with a stone,
> And, hanging in the heavens,
> Out of my boot-top I cast a knife
> At the speechless tremors. (I, 291)

The poem "Razboinik" ("The Outlaw") signaled his readiness
to do battle with typical peasant vaunting: "We have only to
wish it and we'll get everything / On a dark night on the
meadow" (I, 300).

This poetic exuberance would reach its epitome in "Inoniia."
For a moment in his poem "Prishestvie" ("The Coming"), the
vision seemed endangered by betrayal. But "Transfiguration"
was at hand for it was time for God to calve. Earlier imagery
surfaced again, sometimes itself transfigured in the process, as
when the moon suddenly gave birth to a golden pup ("Song
about a Dog," II, 14). The fear of passing Christ by unawares
returned to haunt him (II, 18). His poems read like prayers
addressed to the Mother of God. The new moon, a russet foal,
was ready to take him to his destination: "The ruddy new moon,
becoming a foal / Harnessed itself to our sleigh" (II, 27). The
bridal motif emerged once again: "I would like to press my
body against / The bare breasts of the birches" (II, 28). He
repeated his belief in happiness (II, 29). And his bride became
his muse as both of them went out into the fields of springtime,
as he rejoiced that she had grown stronger and infused in him
a sense of spiritual rebirth—"Because you have grown stronger, /
Because you have filled my soul / With a joyous feast" (II, 30).
In his poem "Metchta" ("Vision," II, 32–34), subtitled "From a
Book of Poems about Love," he heard her calling him; in words
that brought to mind his earlier poem "No more wandering,
no more trampling in the purple bushes," he spoke of his life-
long pursuit of his vision: "But I have always austerely guarded
within me / The gentle curve of your dreamlike arms" (II, 32).
In this series of four poems Esenin was perhaps closest in
perception and tone to Blok's "Poems to the Beautiful Lady" and
the mystic philosopher Vladimir Solovev's "Three Meetings" of
1895 (e.g., his lines "You entered under dark cover / And,

languishing, stood at the window," or "Once I entered into a
white church: / ... / Like a monk, I stood in the scarlet radiance"
(II, 33). In the third poem, as later in Blok, she suffered deformation, appearing as a toothless old hag. But in the fourth his
vision had been restored to him:

> But again you came out of the mist
> And were beautiful and fair.
> Motioning with your arm, you whispered:
> "See how young I am.
> It was life using me to frighten you
> But I am all like air and water."   (II, 34)

IV   "Inoniia"

All of Esenin's expectations burst forth and were "realized"—
at least poetically—in his poem "Inoniia" of 1918, which he
somewhat self-consciously dedicated to the prophet Jeremiah,
with whom, it would seem, he had many poetic and psychological traits in common.[2] "Inoniia" is composed of four parts. In
the first, Esenin, donning the mantle of a new prophet, rejected
Christ in favor of his own vision of a Russian peasant paradise
on earth. It is noteworthy that when he "spat out" Christ's body,
he used the neutral word *Khristos*, and not the more emotionally
charged, popular term *Spas*. His rejection was equivalent to a
renunciation of historical Christianity, with its "bearing of the
Cross." Esenin's vision was life-affirming, this-worldly, and not
disfigured by death: "I have seen another coming / Where Death
does not dance on truth" (II, 37). He carried his iconoclasm and
blasphemy into the second part, when he challenges even God
himself:

> I'll even pluck out God's beard, yea!
> With the baring of my teeth.
>
> I'll catch hold of his white mane,
> Tell him in the voice of the snowstorm:
> I shall make you into another
> So that my word-bearing meadow can ripen!   (II, 37–38)

It was not that Esenin wanted to do away with God altogether; he wanted only to remake him so that his poetry could
grow and flourish. In other words, Esenin's theomachism was
to enable him to continue and realize his poetic vision. Confi-
dently he proclaimed his city of "Inoniia," where peasant man
would be divine: "I promise you the city Inoniia, / Where the god
of the living reigns" (II, 38). This rustic would, with new faith
and strength, furrow the night with the sun. Like the ancient
Jews in Babylonian captivity, the Russian peasant had for too
many years longed for his homeland: "We were weeping on
Babylon's rivers / And a bloody rain soaked us all" (II, 39). The
new god about to be born was a peasant god: "Over our vault-
ing heavens / A god is about to calve" (II, 39). There was no
escape for the Russian Orthodox multitudes who would reject
him: "Still, he'll calve a new sun / For our Russian land" (II,
39). With hyperbolic imagery, Esenin tried to communicate the
inevitable coming of this Russian peasant utopia:

> With the tongs of my hands I'll claw into
> Both poles that are snowy-horned.
>
> With my knee I'll press down the equator,
> And to the moaning of storms and winds
> Into halves I'll break earth-mother
> Like one breaks a golden loaf.   (II, 40)

In part three he carried the battle to America, which for him
symbolized the atheistic, urban world of iron and steel that was
the antipode to his vision:

> Let me warn you, America,
> Split-off half of our globe:
> Don't set out on godless oceans
> In your iron ships!   (II, 40)

It was in this part especially that Esenin's poetic power rose to
unparalleled heights:

> Through free Ladoga waters only
> Can man's passage beyond life be renewed!

> Don't with your blue hands hammer
> Heaven's vault into wastelands far!
> The heads of your nails will never
> Be the glimmer of distant stars.   (II, 40–41)

The world of iron could never measure up to nature. Man could renew and redeem his passage through time only with "free Ladoga waters," that is, through religious, spiritual quest. The world America stood for might destroy his "new Olympian," but then he, Esenin, becoming godlike, would wreak vengeance, devastate America, and in its place create his new paradise:

> New pines shall rise up
> On the palms of your fields.
> And yellow springtimes caper
> Like squirrels on the branches of days.   (II, 42)

The fourth part is a poetic evocation of his peasant Inoniia, a celebration of a new Nazareth—"A new saviour riding on a mare / Is coming to the peasant's world" (II, 44).

V   Rising Disillusionment

Esenin would never come closer to realizing his vision than in this, the most futuristic of his poems. Increasing disillusionment was to mark his poetic path, until in early 1922 his trip abroad provided him with a reprieve.

His poems in "Sel'skii chasoslov" ("Rural Psalter," 1918) pointed to one of the first pronounced breaks in his poetic vision. Now he experienced difficulty in getting to heaven: "Every day / ... / I clamber up to heaven" (II, 47). His vision was being torn to shreds—"My lips sing in blood ... / Snows, white snows / Tear the cover over my native region / To pieces" (II, 47). It should be noted that it was not Christ, but she, his vision, his *rodina* (native land) that hung crucified: "Her body / Hangs on the cross" (II, 48). He had lost his vision, and his native earth (II, 48). With surprising humility, he perceived his personal, intellectual, and perhaps even poetic insignificance in the cosmos when he asked "What can we know, / Shepherds of the desert that we are." But it was better to perish than to be "stripped of one's skin," to abandon one's belief in the coming rebirth of peasant Russia.

In "Iordanskaia golubitsa" ("The Jordanian Dove," 1918) Esenin saw Russia as having cast off from shore on its way to paradise. This is almost the only poem in which Esenin seems to have genuinely claimed that he was a Bolshevik, and that he was prepared to sacrifice his country for the sake of universal brotherhood. It was equally clear, however, that he accepted the Bolshevik utopia on his own, peasant terms. The moon, becoming the shepherd St. Andrew—one of Russia's patron saints—guarded a herd of dun steeds in the vastness of the heavens, amid the golden meadows of Esenin's dreams (II, 56). The dove, symbolic of Christ's baptism and thus the coming of a new age, was on its way to paradise, borne in the palm of the prophetic wind (II, 57).

The doubt that had troubled Esenin in 1916 had returned. At midnight, a white angel had led the poet's steed away, and taken his poetic power with it (II, 62). He felt that his soul was beggared, that his songs were becoming raucous (II, 63). In a curious poem, "Ne stanu nikakuyu" ("I won't [be sweet] to any," 1918), which reflected a desperate stubbornness of vision, the Mother of God herself steps out of the icon to give suck to the poet and sustain him (though the text is ambiguous, it strongly suggests that the infant is in fact the poet). Obstinately, almost wilfully, Esenin defended his right to dream: "I am free to think within, / Spring sings in my soul" (II, 66). Like an old maple on one leg, he stood guard over his vision of light blue Russia (II, 75). But the one-legged image already suggested that he and his vision had been crippled. And in a beautiful poem of 1919 dedicated to Klyuev, he registered that poet's disillusionment and, by inference, his own as well:

> You have given your heart in song to the peasant hut
> But have not built a house in your own heart.
> . . . .
> Oh friend, for whom then did you gild
> Your sources with tuneful word?
>
> You will not be able to sing about the sun,
> Nor see paradise through the window.

> Just as a windmill, flapping its wing,
> Cannot take off from earth.   (II, 76)

The one-winged windmill, like a bird that could not fly, reiterated the "crippled" condition of his poetic state.

As in 1916, he could still rally his creative forces momentarily (here undoubtedly his nascent association with the "Imaginists" must be taken into account). Thus, in the poem "Zakruzhilas' listva zolotaia" ("Golden leaves have started whirling," 1918) he was suddenly full of his previous anticipations of paradise: "As if an airy swarm of butterflies / Were anxiously flying toward a star" (II, 77). The bridal motif, this time with suggestive sexual overtones, recurred:"The youthful wind has blown the birch's skirt / Up to its very shoulders" (II, 77). He confessed that he had never before listened with such attention to the wisdom of the flesh (II, 77). In the last stanza of this poem he reverted to his early imagery to express his final spiritual satisfaction, although in a subjunctive and interrogative sense:

> It would be nice to be the new moon's face
> To smile at a haystack and chew its hay . . .
> Where are you my quiet joy
> Of loving everything and desiring nothing?   (II, 78)

A number of poems reflected his intent to wait patiently and sustain his poetic inspiration while being, animallike, in heat:

> In my heart I am learning how to keep
> The color of bird-cherries in my eyes,
> Only avariciously can feelings be warmed,
> When the animal in heat breaks one's ribs.   (II, 79)

After this, Esenin's poetry became much more desperate, as in his longer poem "Pantokrator" ("Pantocrator," 1919). This work continued the iconoclasm of "Inoniia," but in a much more tenderly filial, if still crude, vein:

> Lord, you have taught me not how to pray to you
> But how to rail at you.

It is because of your curly grey hair
And the copecks from the golden trembling poplars
That I shout to you: "To hell with the old!"
Unruly and outlaw son of yours that I am.   (II, 82)

The very first stanza sets the tone for his desperation—

Let him who howls and raves
Who buries his yearning in his shoulder praise my poetry,
And him who tries to catch hold of the new moon's horse face
By its bridle of light.   (II, 82)

This was a last attempt to clutch the reins of the moon-steed
and be off on his journey. Yet, even here, in the first two lines
of the stanza, he dedicated his poetry to those who would gather
in his Moscow taverns and give vent to precisely this rage and
yearning that the political revolution had first fostered, then
later ignored and betrayed. The spectacle he had witnessed in
a Moscow street of a hungry dog tearing away at a horse's
carcass while two crows feasted on the eyes of another horse,
gave him the imagery of his poetic predicament in the poem
"Kobyl'i korabli ("Mares' Ships," 1919). A wolf howled at a
star, the heavens were chewed up by clouds, mares' bellies
were ripped open, and the wings of ravens that sat on them
resembled black sails going nowhere (II, 87). The revolution he
had enthusiastically welcomed was no longer his revolution:
it would never reach paradise, for paradise could not be attained
with hacked-off arms for oars: "With hacked-off arms for oars /
You are rowing to the land of the future" (II, 87). Windows
broken and doors left ajar combine in a vision of uninhabited
desolation, when even the sun froze like a puddle of urine left
behind by a gelding. Poetic energy was dwindling. On the
roads hungry dogs sucked at the edge of twilight. How, he
asked, could he go on singing in a world mad with war and
destruction (II, 88). Even his bridal vision was degraded to
one of the poet marrying a ewe in a barn (II, 89). The political
revolution, "evil October," was ripping the fingers from the
brown hands of birches, was desecrating and mutilating his
vision (II, 89). His last refuge was the world of nature into
which he had once been born on St. John's Eve, the animal
world that alone now could share his rage and suffering. He

would rather die with his "sister bitches and brother dogs" than advance with people. He would not cast a stone at his mad fellow man, but his rejection of humankind here poetically fore-shadowed the poem "Wolf's End." Soon autumn, the wise gardener, would cut off his head like a yellow leaf; there was only one path into the twilight garden, and the October wind was about to bare the groves, strip and "rape" his bridal vision (II, 90). The only solution seemed for his poetry, almost sui-cidally, to cut deeper: "Cut deeper, sickles of poetry!" (II, 90).

He yearned for his once pure and innocent vision in "Vetry, vetry, o snezhnye vetry," ("Winds, winds, oh snowy winds," 1919), where he symbolized his pain and himself in the image of a tree during a raging snowstorm: "Like a tree I would like to stand / By the road on one leg alone" (II, 91). In "Po-osennemu kychet sova" ("As in autumn the owl is hooting," 1920), the self-sacrificial note of the preceding poem is muted into resig-nation. He knew that a new poet would replace him, that he, Esenin, would grow cold and leafless. Young and old in the vil-lage would sing without him. In poignant lines he described the approach of poetic impotence:

> I'll have to grow old, leafless
> Fill my ears with the sound of stars.
> Without me young men will sing verses,
> Not to me will the old men hark.   (II, 92)

In his "Prayer for the Dead" of 1920, the young foal's failure to outrun the train unmistakably indicated that both he and his poetry were out of place, and had been left behind by urban civilization. The offensive and indecent "Imaginist" imagery of this poem only emphasized the agony and anger of defeat. Even the windmill had grown old, and would never take wing. His village, its very life, lay in a coma and delirium: "The life of these wooden peasant huts / Is being shaken by steel fever" (II, 94). The poem's third part burst out in tenderness toward this "silly" foal, and, by extension, toward the rural existence that it represented (II, 95). At the end of the poem the rowanberry bush, symbolic of erotic and spiritual fulfill-ment, had crushed its head in against a wattle fence (II, 96).

In "Ia poslednii poet derevni" ("I'm the last village poet,"

1920), the once promising imagery of birches symbolized, not a future meeting, but a leave taking by the last village poet: "I witness the farewell liturgy / Of birches scattering their leaves like incense" (II, 97). His songs could not survive the advent of the "iron guest." Only nature would mourn him: "Only the grain-eared steeds / Will recall their old master and grieve" (II, 98).

Before writing his dramatic poems "Pugachev" (1921), and "Wolf's End" (1922), Esenin composed a number of poems expressing his idealistic rebelliousness in the guise of "hooliganism." In "Khuligan" ("The Hooligan," 1920), he saw himself as sole bard and witness of old Russia, built of wood (II, 99). But he also saw himself as a captive of his vision, doomed to the melancholy of his animallike poems, sentenced to emotional hard labor (II, 99–100). That he visualized himself as a "hooligan," as a robber in the night waiting for his prey, suggests that his vision was now socially "outcast," that he could only achieve it under cover of night. In this respect the poem was a poetic precursor of "Pugachev." In "Ispoved' Khuligana" ("Confession of a Hooligan," 1920), he commented that it was not given him to drop, like an apple, before strangers' feet (II, 101). He might wear a top hat and lacquered shoes, but he had never ceased to love his native countryside (II, 101–102). Though he seemed "urbanized," in his heart he still nourished the remembrance of his childhood, he was still the same, his eyes still bloomed like cornflowers in the rye (II, 103). And his will was still left to him. Using the image of a yellow sail, possibly developed out of "Mares' Ships," he avowed his desire to follow his (and his peasant brethren's) course to the end: "I want to be a yellow sail / Going to the land whither we are sailing" (II, 104). But in the poem "Pesn' o khlebe" ("Song about Bread," 1921), the erstwhile sheaves of wheat that had promised plenty and fulfillment looked more like yellow corpses; and the windmill that ground them to flour was another windmill altogether (II, 105-106).

VI *"Pugachev" and "Wolf's End"*

Esenin worked out his poetic dilemma in the narrative poem "Pugachev" of 1921. This was, therefore, in creative terms, a highly significant poem for him, which explains the bitterness with which he reacted to hostile criticism of it. But the critics were right when they pointed to the lyrical and subjective—not historical—epic quality of "Pugachev," and to its sometimes heavily ornate imagery. Perhaps this in itself suggested the burden under which Esenin-Pugachev labored.

It is fairly obvious to any reader who comes to "Pugachev" from the body of Esenin's earlier poetry that the Cossack leader of the eighteenth century uprising againt Catherine the Great, Emiliyan Pugachev, was in reality Esenin personified. Thus, at the very outset of the poem, Pugachev is preoccupied with the destruction of the old Russian village way of life, and the fate of the Russian peasant (IV, 160). Furthermore, if Pugachev was Esenin, Catherine could, by the same token, stand for the Bolsheviks. For instance, the night watchman's words to Pugachev to the effect that the peasant no longer controlled the fruits of his agricultural labor and that all of Russia groaned beneath her treacherous hold (IV, 161) may be interpreted in a more contemporary sense. To Pugachev's question whether the Russian peasant is capable of revolt, the night watchman answers in images reminiscent of Part III of "Prayer for the Dead," images that suggest Esenin's own spiritual predicament, caught as he was between village and city, between the worlds of nature and of iron, on a road inundated by birches' tears (IV, 161–62). At the outset, Esenin conveys the idea of the betrayal of the vision of a just society, and the threat to its realization, in Pugachev's image of stars, like teeth, being one by one pulled out of the darkness by the tongs of twilight (IV, 163).

The yearning for a new life by peasants and Cossacks alike— the words of the character Kirpichnikov echo Esenin's paradisal vision—was expressed in their desire, if only their huts had wheels, to harness horses to them and be off "To a new region, to live a new life" (IV, 167). The impossibility of huts on wheels recalls the inertia of such images as Esenin's one-winged windmill. Still, Kirpichnikov and his men choose to rise up against the representatives of Catherine's power (IV, 167–68). And if, in the next scene, the Cossack sentry Karavaev would gladly flee his strife-torn land (IV, 170)—anticipating, perhaps, the bandit leader Nomakh's successful escape from Soviet Russia in the

dramatic poem "Strana negodiaev" ("The Land of Scoundrels," 1922–1923), or even Esenin's own departure abroad in
the spring of 1922—the lyrical, nature-oriented Pugachev decides
to fight rather than flee (IV, 173).

Pugachev reputedly sought vengeance for Catherine's murder of her husband, Peter III (IV, 174), but, in pretending
to be Peter III, Pugachev is by implication also avenging Esenin, whom he personifies. In this sense it is not surprising to
find Pugachev alluding to the luckless seven pups of "Song
about a Dog," when he remarks that his vengeance has been
born of "bloody pups" (IV, 175). Esenin's own poetic and social
dilemma is reflected in Pugachev's cry of anguish over the impossibility of being himself:

> It is painful for me to be Peter
> When my blood and soul belong to Emeliyan.
> Man in this world is not a wooden house,
> You cannot always rebuild it according to a new plan.   (IV, 177)

Esenin also personified himself in Khlopusha, a peasant's son,
a former convict, an audacious scoundrel and crook, as he calls
himself, the personification of vengeance itself (IV, 181). As
he seeks Pugachev, his words to the sentries echo Esenin's bridal
vision, except that now the imagery has cooled and become
coarser, more "bestial":

> Like a ruddy she-camel the Orenburg dawn
> Let its twilight milk pour into my mouth.
> And through the murk I pressed its cold, rough udder
> To my exhausted eyelids, as one would with bread.
> Take me, take me to him.
> I want to see that man.   (IV, 178)

Like the poet, Khlopusha too has been carrying an unbearable
spiritual burden: "I carried my soul, heavier than stones" (IV,
179). And, in a reminiscence of "Wolf's End," Khlopusha
compares himself to a wolf ready to feed on human flesh (IV,
181). The character Tornov also expresses Esenin's sense of
poetic and spiritual doom in an image of the moon-steed of yore
transformed into a rotting horse skull (IV, 184). Recalling the
poem "Prayer for the Dead," the image of chimney riders astride

Russian huts that, with their ornamental, horse-headed gable roofs, looked like a wild herd of wooden mares galloping who knows where (IV, 185), once again suggests the inertia of Esenin's poetic vision. Zarubin, another of the poet's alter egos, tries to sound an optimistic note: "Not misfortune, but unexpected joy / Will fall on old peasant Russia," he says (IV, 186). But Pugachev's army is defeated; Khlopusha is killed, and Zarubin imprisoned. Ruin has come (IV, 188). It remains for Burnov, another of Pugachev's followers, to express Esenin's agonizing yearning for creative life: "I want to live, live, live, / Even if it means terror and pain," (IV, 189). Burnov's voice is unmistakably Esenin's as he cries out that he would do all and anything if someone would only teach him how to "sound in the garden of man" (IV, 189).

This love of life in a negative sense is also shared by Tvorogov "For we live but once, only once" (IV, 190)—though he ends by betraying Pugachev and his cause. Pugachev's hope of escaping into Asia to regroup his forces (IV, 192) foreshadows Esenin's later yearning to get out to Persia. But it was too late. As Pugachev is being disarmed by traitors, he hears someone's secret, hostile snigger (IV, 195), which suggests Tvorogov's titter.

It is consonant with Esenin's poetic perception that Pugachev himself sees autumn as the real traitor. Since the word for "autumn" in Russian is feminine in gender, Pugachev extends the meaning of the metaphor to mean "she, who had betrayed him." In this way Esenin connects Pugachev's downfall (and his own) with the bridal theme. As had sometimes been the case in his earlier poems, she, his vision, has now become a base and vicious old woman:

> It is she
> Who has bribed you,
> That evil, mean, ragged old hag.
> It is she, she, she
> Who, having scattered her hair in unsteady twilight
> Wants our native country to be ruined
> Under her cheerless, cold smile.   (IV, 195)

Tvorogov and his henchmen of course fail to comprehend the poetic allusion, and Tvorogov exclaims that this is the end of

Pugachev's furious, wolfish howling (IV, 195). Pugachev's mono-
logue at the poem's conclusion expresses the poetic impotence,
the exhaustion of imaginative, creative power, the spiritual and
visionary disillusionment that Esenin himself must have felt:
"Is it possible that the end has come? / Is it possible that one
falls under the soul's weight as one would under a burden?"
(IV, 196). Spiritual burdens could also crush one in the end.

Esenin's poem "Wolf's End" (1922) simply and tragically re-
enacts, in a poetically more compressed form, this "falling
under the weight of a spiritual burden," using the figure of a
wolf, an animal dear to Esenin. Equally dear to him was the
ancient, mysterious village world now being throttled to death
by stone roads, those extensions of the city. But he was ready to
meet his "dark hour of ruin," for he recognized the "sinewy,"
devilish power that stemmed from the city. The wolf's encir-
clement by hunters symbolizes Esenin's creative dilemma and
his precarious social condition as a lyrical rustic poet. Like
"Pugachev," "Wolf's End" defines the extent of his poetic and
social alienation from the "urban" world of the Soviets. The
circle tightens until the identification between poet and wolf
is complete:

> Oh, greetings to you, best-loved animal!
> Not for nothing do you yield to the blow.
> Like you I'm hunted everywhere,
> And pass through iron foes.   (II, 112)

Like the wolf, Esenin would in his last fatal leap, taste of the
enemy's blood, and a song of vengeance would sound for him
"on the other shore." His poetry would avenge him.

Although Esenin's Imagist period, especially after 1917, was
a creatively intensive one, his imagery of the years between
1918 and early 1922 showed only too clearly his mounting
despair, which was directly proportional to the spiritual effort
he expended to sustain a poetic vision in a revolutionary world
that had grown increasingly hostile to his lyrical sensibility. The
road to paradise seemed beset by insurmountable obstacles, the
call of his muse kept receding before him, until his poems
"Pugachev" and "Wolf's End" signaled the entire hopelessness

of his situation, the spiritual weariness of an impossible pilgrimage. One might add that his best poems (critics later noted
something similar in connection with his *Tavern Moscow* poems)
were those that expressed his anguish. As he had put it in his
letter of August 1920 to Evgeniya Livshits, the socialism he
had imagined had indeed nothing in common with the "deliberate" one he saw rising all around him.

CHAPTER 5

To the West and Back

I Europe and America

E SENIN met and impressed the famous dancer Isadora Duncan (1878–1927) in early November 1921.[1] The Soviet writer Ilya Ehrenburg wrote of their relationship that Duncan's "love enchanted him as a mark of universal recognition."[2] Sergey Gorodetsky has written that theirs was a deep and mutual love. Esenin, he remarks, was of course as much in love with her fame as he was with her, but then women did not play the great role in his life that they did, say, in Blok's. For Esenin, falling in love was one of the most unimportant aspects of his life.[3] There was something fated, Anatoly Mariengof felt, in Esenin's inexplicable, enormous need to meet a woman he had never seen, and a woman who, though a great person and an exceptionally gifted artist, would be such a destructive influence in his life.[4] M. Babenchikov, on the other hand, maintained that Isadora exerted a positive influence on Esenin. She understood the poet in him, and tried in her own original fashion to lighten the despair that was noticeably growing within him. Babenchikov saw their meeting as an experience that made a profound impact on the poet's life. He recalls that, in early 1922, Esenin often lacked the strength to conceal his state of inner fear, anxiety, and alarm.[5] Ivan Startsev, though, has noted Esenin's two-faced attitude toward Isadora. In public he could be all attention, totally in love with her. In private, he sometimes abused and mistreated her.[6]

Before Isadora and Esenin left for abroad, they were married in Moscow on May 2, 1922. The idea of going abroad had been Isadora's. She wanted to show him "all that Europe had of beauty, and all that America had of wonder." She also felt he

61

was a "very sick man." They left Russia on May 10, 1922.[7]

Their first stop was Berlin. Ehrenburg recalled:

In Berlin I saw him several times with Isadora Duncan. She realized what a terribly hard time he was going through, wanted to help and could not. She was almost twice his age and had not only great talent, but also humanity, tenderness, and tact. But he was a nomad, a gypsy; nothing frightened him so much as the thought of being emotionally settled.[8]

It was also in Berlin that Esenin suffered a nervous breakdown, as a result of which he could hardly move one of his legs.[9] In a letter of June 21, 1922, Esenin wrote to a correspondent: "The Berlin atmosphere strained my nerves to the utmost. Because of my shattered nerves, I can scarcely drag my foot now. I am being treated in Wiesbaden. I have stopped drinking and have begun to work."[10]

After stopping off in Paris and Venice, they sailed for the United States, arriving in New York on October 1, 1922.[11] After some initial difficulty in entering the country because Isadora was suspected of being a Soviet agent, they stayed four months, during which time Duncan gave performances in the major U.S. cities. The problems that beset them are described in Irma Duncan's and Allan Ross Macdougall's book on Isadora:

Then, at the end of the month, wearied by the press campaign waged against her, worried by the state of her husband's mental and physical health, which his unfortunate experience with bootleg liquor had done nothing to ameliorate, penniless to the point of having to borrow the fare . . . she sailed. . . .[12]

They were back in Paris in February:

The arrival in Paris, back in Europe, was too much for Essenine. He attempted at once to drown all his memories of America in wine, or rather vodka. But the alcohol imbibed with such Slavic gluttony, instead of bringing forgetfulness, roused all the demons within him. Like a maniac he rushed into his chamber at the Crillon Hotel one night and smashed all the mirrors and the woodwork. With difficulty he was mastered by the police and led off to the nearest "poste."[13]

Several influential friends helped obtain Esenin's release. Subsequent developments forced Isadora to have Esenin moved to a private mental hospital. A return to Russia seemed in Esenin's best interests. By August 5, 1923, they were back in Moscow.[14]

In his autobiography written in that same year, Esenin claimed that he was pleased most of all to be back in Soviet Russia.[15] But in a letter he had written to his friend Alexander Kusikov while on his way back to Paris, on February 7, 1923, he had said the exact opposite:

Sandro, Sandro! I feel a deadly and unendurable anguish and dejection, I feel myself a stranger here and not needed. But when I think of Russia and what awaits me there, then I don't even want to go back. If I were alone, if I had no sisters, I would spit on it all and go off to Africa or some place else. I feel sick and disgusted at the thought that I, a rightful son of Russia, should be a step-son in my own country. I've had enough of that filthily sluttish and condescending attitude of those in power, and I'm even more disgusted when I have to endure the servile flattery shown them by my very own writing fraternity. I can't endure it anymore! Honest to God I can't. The only thing left to do would be to scream for help or get hold of a knife and take to the highway.[16]

He confessed that a "vicious gloom" had descended upon him: "I cease to understand which revolution I had belonged to. I only see that apparently it was neither the February nor the October one."[17]

On the other hand, he was genuinely disenchanted with the West. The letters Esenin sent from abroad to his friends in Russia suggest as much.[18] Indecent poetry like his had no chance whatsoever amidst German orderliness, he complained. He would like to return to Russia, away from the nightmare that was Europe, back to his former youthful hooliganism and enthusiasm. He experienced boredom and lonely yearning in Europe. Nor did he feel any different about the United States. He wrote Mariengof from New York that the city was so abominable as to invite suicide. He was afraid that he might lose the love and spiritual sense of his art, in which no one seemed interested here. He felt utterly useless.[19] Before going back to Russia, his

only positive recollection of his sojourn in the West was his boast
that he had "beaten and smashed" both Europe and America.[20]

II *Return and Death*

On August 5, 1923, Isadora and Esenin returned to Moscow;
they almost immediately began to drift apart. Isadora departed
for a tour of the Caucasus. After the end of October, Esenin
dropped out of her life. She remained in Russia until September
30, 1924.[21] Esenin was later to admit that Isadora had really
loved him.[22]

Georgy Ustinov recalls that on his return from abroad Esenin
was in a depressed emotional state. He had aged, and looked
lost. He spoke of Germany and France only with malice. Ustinov
suggests that the reason for this attitude lay in the fact that his
anticipation of a triumphant procession across Europe had been
sorely disappointed. In fact, Esenin admitted to Ustinov, he had
behaved scandalously abroad as a means of attracting attention.
Ustinov stressed Esenin's sense of isolation at that point, his
gnawing feeling that nobody loved him.[23]

The Marxist critic Alexander Voronsky (1884–1943), editor of
the journal *Krasnaia nov'* (*Red Virgin Soil*), met Esenin in the
autumn of 1923. In his recollections of the poet, he wrote that
Esenin was dressed so as to create an unusual impression of ele-
gance at a time when most people still had not contrived to
clean themselves up. Esenin wore makeup, his eyelids were
swollen, and his eyes were dull. He had a touch of that Russian
contemplative sadness about him, comments Voronsky: he drank,
and had no desire to write.[24] In a half-jesting, half-serious manner, Esenin said to him as he was leaving Voronsky's office:
"Let's work together and be friends. But keep in mind: I know
you're a communist. I'm also for Soviet power, but I love old
Russia (*Rus'*). I go my own way. I won't allow you to muzzle
me and I won't dance to a tune. Nothing will come of that."[25]

On another occasion, Voronsky saw Esenin on a wintry night
in 1923 or 1924 near the "Stall of Pegasus," as he was getting
out of a sleigh. He wore a top hat and a Pushkinian cape. When
Voronsky inquired about this masquerade, Esenin replied—like
a capricious, offended child—that he wanted to resemble Pushkin, the greatest poet in the world. Then he confessed to Voron-

sky that he was bored.[26] Rozanov remembers how on June 6, 1924—the one hundred twenty-fifth anniversary of Pushkin's birth—Esenin read a poem to honor Pushkin. Rozanov observed that Esenin's poem referred to Pushkin's "blondish" hair, an attempt by Esenin to have Pushkin resemble him.[27] Prehaps Esenin's many jaunts to the Caucasus during 1924 and 1925 fulfilled some similar urge to follow in Pushkin's footsteps. The writer Ivan Rakhillo has suggested that Esenin's belief in the mighty power of poetry over human hearts was linked to his veneration for Pushkin.[28] It is not surprising, then, to learn that, a few weeks before his death, Esenin reread Pushkin's letters and was enraptured by them.[29]

Esenin's physical and mental state was aggravated by still other factors. He suffered from *delirium tremens,* an acute case of alcoholism that, according to one observer, he "inherited" from his father and grandfather.[30] The poet Nikolay Tikhonov recalled meeting Esenin in Tbilisi once; Esenin complained to him about his sleepless nights, and about grey birds and bats that kept flying into his room, sitting on his bedstead or hanging in the window.[31] Esenin suffered from hallucinations and a persecution complex; he believed people were plotting to do away with him.[32] In this connection his long poem "The Black Man," on which he worked during the last years of his life, while he was abroad, is of interest.[33] We know that Esenin read it to Maxim Gorky in Italy in 1923, and that Gorky wept.[34] The psychiatrist I. B. Galant, who analyzed the poem in 1926 from a medical and clinical point of view, concluded that the poem demonstrated beyond any doubt that Esenin was mentally ill.[35] This would mean that Esenin was already in a deranged mental state when he went abroad, and that Isadora Duncan was justified in considering him "a very sick man" in need of special care. Ivnev has even suggested that Esenin was a cocaine addict.[36] Others have claimed that he smoked opium in the summer of 1924 in Baku.[37] He made several unsuccessful suicide attempts.[38] Esenin was also deeply shaken by the death of his friend, the poet Alexander Shiryaevets, on May 15, 1924: he maintained it was a suicide.[39] Startsev remembers how Esenin came to him with the tragic news, fell on the couch and sobbed that it was time for him too to prepare to follow that same path.[40]

In the last two years of life, Esenin seemed possessed by a force beyond his control, ever restless and unable to find spiritual anchorage. His friend, the writer Sofya Vinogradskaya, says of this last period that Esenin was searching for refuge and human warmth. To her he seemed as helpless as a two year old child. He could not organize his own life. He was forever surrounded by hangers-on who wanted only money from him, and who exploited his need for friendship and flattered his poetic ego.

Galina Benislavskaya became his most devoted friend at this point (she herself committed suicide over Esenin's grave in December 1926).[41] Esenin had been in touch with her as early as October 1921, and then again in September 1923, when he married her.[42] According to Vinogradskaya, Esenin settled down with Benislavskaya in the summer of 1924 at a time when he was still in touch with Isadora (it should be noted that their marriage was never dissolved) and often terrified that she might come for him. He seemed to be afraid of something. But he took care of his sisters and encouraged beginning poets.

Benislavskaya sacrificed herself for Esenin. She became wife, friend, sister, and mother to him. She worried over him, published his poems, obtained money for him and generally looked after him. And yet Esenin underestimated her devotion, Vinogradskaya writes. He only realized the loss when they parted.[43]

Vinogradskaya found Esenin also deeply vexed that all his feelings seemed to go into his poetry, and did not exist apart from it. He could not live without writing, she says. When he wrote he was sober, but in the intervals he drank and felt bored. Vinogradskaya saw him again in the summer of 1925, before his departure for the Caucasus, when he was married to Sofia Tolstaya. His eyes reflected an inner torment, and he spoke as if they might never see each other again.[44]

The poet Volf Erlikh has described the last two years of Esenin's life. Esenin confessed to him that he had spent his personal life in vain for something "which I don't have now." The crux of the matter seems to have been Esenin's waning poetic powers: he admitted that he was beginning to write verse instead of poetry.[45]

The poet Vasily Nasedkin has written specifically on Esenin's last year of life. This year, more than any other, says Nasedkin, was marked by unsuccessful poetry readings. In February of 1925, Esenin had just returned from Baku*, bringing with him his *Persidskie motivy* (Persian Motifs) poems and "Anna Snegina." It was also in February (actually March) that he met Tolstaya, Leo Tolstoy's granddaughter. From March to November Esenin, like one pursued, moved feverishly between Moscow, the Caucasus, Konstantinovo, and back to Moscow, and began to drink again. In early June he left Benislavskaya. He sold the rights to his collected works to the State Publishing House on June 20, and wanted to use the money either to go abroad to visit Gorky or to return to the Caucasus. (He declined to enter a sanatorium in Germany, as his family and close friends wished him to.)[46] His nerves were completely shattered from drinking. He married Tolstaya. Esenin freely acknowledged that he was seeking destruction. By the end of November, when Esenin finally entered a clinic, his persecution mania had intensified, and his hallucinations became more frequent. He drank for days on end, so that friends began to avoid him. Suddenly, on December 21, he left the clinic, drank for two days, and went off to Leningrad, intending to work, to get married again, to start a journal, to visit Gorky abroad.[47] Startsev recalls the terror in Esenin's eyes as he told him of a girl who had hanged herself by her own braid in the clinic.[48]

Both Erlikh and Ustinov's wife, Elizaveta Ustinova, have described Esenin's last four days in Leningrad. Esenin went to the Hotel d'Angleterre, where the Ustinovs were also staying. He went to see Klyuev, whom, Esenin said, he still loved and respected as his teacher. But Klyuev commented that Esenin's latest poems would make up a nice little book for the reading of all the maidens and tender youths of Russia. Esenin talked of suicide and wrote a poem in his own blood because he had no ink, or so he said. He read "The Black Man" to a small

---

* In 1924 and 1925 Esenin went to the Caucasus (Baku, Batum, Tbilisi) on several occasions. He felt close to the literary world of Georgia and became acquainted with leading Georgian poets. He even dedicated one of his poems to them (IV, 207–10). Esenin actually returned to Moscow on March 1 after a prolonged stay in the Caucasus.

group of friends. Then, on the morning of December 28, Erlikh and Ustinova found him hanging from the waterpipe in his room.[49]

Ustinova remembered that, two days before his suicide, Esenin had told her he was bored with life and did not need anyone or anything. He spoke of himself as "God's reed." When she asked him to explain, he said that he meant by that a man who had spent freely from his treasure house and never replenished it because he had nothing to return, nor was he even interested in doing so. He was just such a man, Esenin said. Ustinova was certain Esenin committed suicide while in a mentally deranged state.[50]

As Galant saw it, Esenin died by his own hand because the poet in him refused to adjust to life as it was, with all its baseness, which offended his higher poetic instincts. He failed to resolve this inner conflict and, what is worse, the accompanying decline in his psychic powers, in life energy, led to a further creative decline. Without creative genius, life for him was not worth living.[51] As Gorodetsky phrased it in his reminiscences of the poet:

I acknowledge the truth of the words of Anatoly Mariengof, Esenin's closest friend during his most conscious period of life: "If Sergey decided to leave us, he must have somehow come to doubt his own creative powers. There could not be any other reason for his death, just as he had no other aim in life save his poems."[52]

CHAPTER 6

Last Period

IN his last period, Esenin became an increasingly broken man, headed for a physical, mental, and creative breakdown, especially after his return to the Soviet Union. The twenty-one "Tavern Moscow" poems,[1] eighteen of which were published under the title *Moskva kabatskaia* (*Tavern Moscow*) in 1924, gave full expression to the creative despair Esenin had voiced in his poem "Wolf's End."

I "Tavern Moscow"

He would not deceive himself any longer, Esenin announced in the first of his "Tavern Moscow" poems proper, written in 1922 (II, 119).[2] He harbored no illusions about his personal poetic alienation from Soviet society, and—here he picked up the poetic thread of his vision—he realized that he had subordinated his poetic imagination to the vision of another "kingdom": "I find no friendship among people, / I have submitted to another kingdom" (II, 120). Like the thugs and whores with whom he associated in this tavern world, he felt himself a social outcast condemned by God to die in the "twisted streets of Moscow" (II, 121–22). Amid fighting and weeping, amid the "yellow sorrow" spread by the accordion, this tavern folk looked back to old, Moscovite Russia (II, 123). He himself, the poet, was drowning his vision, his "eyes," in wine (II, 123). The odor of death blended with a sense of something lost by everyone forever. Even the accordion player was a syphilitic. There was something vicious in the "maddened eyes" of these tavern dwellers, something defiant, and yet full of pity for those who—like the poet—had come to ruin: "They pity those young foolish ones / Who have ruined their lives in the heat of passion" (II,

69

124). The poet was overcome by love for this Asiatic Russia. The original fifth stanza of the poem—presumably excluded by Esenin—provided the reason for their anger and defiance: "stern October" had deceived them as it had Esenin, and they were now preparing for resistance (II, 289).

One of the most painful poems in this cycle was "Syp', garmonika. Skuka ... Skuka ..." ("Let's go, accordion. I feel so bored," 1923). Here Esenin's "utopian" vision is utterly deformed. The bride who had once beckoned to him as a vision of paradise was now flesh and blood, but a prostitute sitting and drinking with him, a "filthy bitch." She had been unbearably worn out by others, but he would not commit suicide yet, he added, and suddenly welled over with genuine tenderness for her: "Dear love, I am weeping / Forgive me ... forgive me ..." (II, 126). In his next poem, he realized that this kind of love could be a contagion and plague, that it could make a hooligan lose his senses. Instead of happiness, he had found in her his undoing, for she had deserted him: "I sought happiness in this woman / But instead accidentally found my ruin" (II, 127). Still, he could not curse her; he was still capable of vision: "My heart has a bagful of golden dreams" (II, 128). At the same time, the poem's coarse imagery suggests the depths to which his ideal has sunk: "One by one the male dogs lick / The bitch's bleeding sap" (II, 128).

He could not find the way back to his native village (II, 130). He was painfully aware that he could no longer believe in God, that the darkness of everyday existence had engulfed his vision when his only reason for having been a hooligan and brawler was to burn more brightly:

> I am ashamed that I believed in God,
> And deeply sad that I no longer believe now.
>
> Golden distant spaces!
> Life's worldly events burn everything down.
> All my foul-mouthed brawling
> Was intended to make me burn more brightly.   (II, 131)

In "Ia ustalym takim eshche ne byl" ("Never have I felt so exhausted," 1923?), a worm gnaws away at his eyes as if they were blue leaves (II, 151). He felt so tired that neither betrayal nor easy triumph could touch him. His poetic vision had totally faded: "That hair's golden hay color / Is turning grey" (II, 151). The road to paradise had brought him instead to the tavern: "This straight road / Has brought me to the tavern" (II, 149). In this poem ("Grubym daetsia radost'" ["Rude ones experience joy"], 1923?), there were already touches of "The Black Man," as the poet, Esenin, collected corks from bottles to stop up his soul (II, 150).

Since the deformation of Esenin's poetic ideal in feminine form, symptomatic of the ebbing away of creative energy, characterizes his last period, it is not surprising that Esenin attempted to revitalize the sources of his poetic inspiration through woman (Blok had done essentially the same in his *Snezhnaia maska* [*Snow Mask*] cycle of 1907). This is the function of the "Liubov' Khuligana" ("Love of a Hooligan") cycle of poems, dedicated to the actress Augusta Miklashevskaya.

Yet even here his recurring use of the unreal conditional construction suggested that he could not achieve his objective. This impossibility had less to do with a real, live woman than with her whom she symbolized: "You I would follow forever / Into familiar or unfamiliar regions" (II, 134). That Miklashevskaya in fact symbolized his poetic ideal is also suggested by the lines "You have become twice as pleasing / To my poet's imagination" (II, 137).

But all too suddenly the sorrow and the pain were there again, and the visionary potential of his earthbound female companion had diminished. Some stranger had already possessed her (II, 141). Esenin recorded his present predicament in the image of birches whose bones had been gnawed clean and strewn over a garden resembling a cemetery (II, 142). As her power to inspire him vanished, his soul came to resemble a yellow skeleton in the grip of an epileptic fit (II, 143). All that was left of his Imaginist period was a "shirt front" and a "fashionable pair of worn out boots." He was overripe: "I know that my feeling has become overripe, / And yours won't be able to flower" (II, 144)

That Esenin should have placed a poem written in the spring of 1922 ("Ne zhaleiu, ne zovu, ne plachu," ["I do not regret, do not call, do not weep"]) at the conclusion of his 1924 *Tavern*

Moscow collection suggested how little his poetic condition had
improved in those two years. In this poem he lamented the passing of his youth, and commented that his heart had been touched
by a ripple of cold: "And the land of birches' cotton / Will not
lure me into running barefoot there" (II, 113). His poetic power,
too, was withering:

> More and more rarely the spirit to wander
> Moves my lips' fire.
> Oh, my lost freshness,
> Eyes' tumult and spring torrents flooding my senses.   (II, 113)

Had his vision, his life, been a dream, he asked; was it as if he
had galloped past on a rose-colored steed once in the early
hours of spring? But he found enough strength to bless the
advent and the decline of creative inspiration:

> We are all mortal in this world,
> The leaves' copper silently falls from the maples . . .
> Let what came to flower and die
> Be forever blessed.   (II, 114)

II   *Pushkin*

After his emotive-poetic involvement with woman, Esenin's
"gravitation" toward Pushkin represented perhaps a second,
and equally futile, attempt to regain his poetic footing. But a
reading of his work shows that there is little in his poems of the
time to justify speaking of a "Pushkin" phase in his work. It is
true that Esenin tried in real life to "imitate" and "identify" himself with Pushkin, and his poem "Pushkinu" ("To Pushkin,"
1924), read before Pushkin's statue in Moscow, was designed to
draw physical and autobiographical parallels between himself
and Pushkin (II, 164). But this was no more than a reflection of
his preoccupation with questions of poetic fame and posterity.
Esenin's poetry was incapable of absorbing Pushkin's poetic
impact. If Pushkin had never existed, the tone and Imagist power
of Esenin's poetry would have remained what they were, an organic part of his own poetic world. Occasional poetic references
to Pushkin, a few random quotations from his work, the rare

Pushkinian echo, cannot be taken as proof of anything more
than a superficial "influence" of Pushkin on Esenin's poetry
(see, e.g., his poems "Na Kavkaze" ["In the Caucasus," 1924];
"Poetam Gruzii" ["To the Poets of Georgia," 1924]; or "Pis'mo k
sestre" ["Letter to My Sister," 1925]).

What appeared superficially as Pushkin's "classical" influence
was simply a symptom of poetic decline in Esenin. To take one
indicative instance, he could no longer recast the earthly details
of Russian village life into an envisaged ideal poetic reality:
see, for example, "Etoi grusti teper' ne rassypat'" ("I can no
longer shake off this sorrow now," 1924), and especially his
"Pis'mo ot materi" ("Letter from Mother," 1924), where the
image of the poet became but a foil for the ordinary family man.
Hence his lament that the familiar moonlit landscape had already
lost some of its beauty and appeal: "The spaces familiar to
sight / Are no longer as appealing under the moon" (II, 166);
and "My white linden has finished flowering, / The songs of my
nightingale-filled dawn have died down" (II, 167).

Esenin expressed his uselessness as a poet especially vividly in
"Rus' sovetskaia" ("Soviet *Rus'*," 1924). Here even his one-
winged windmill suddenly became motionless: "Here even the
windmill, that wooden bird, / Stands around with its one wing
and its eyes shut" (II, 168). Like his foal once upon a time, it
was he who now was "silly" (II, 169). On leaving, he would
take only his love for his native soil and his poetry with him,
entrusting the latter neither to revolution, mother, friend, nor
spouse:

> I shall give my soul to October and May,
> Only my dear lyre I'll not give away.
>
> I shall not give it into strangers' hands,
> Nor to mother, friend or wife
> It entrusted its sounds only to me,
> And only to me did it sing its tender songs. (II, 171)

A double allusion to Esenin's feminine source of inspiration may
be contained in the phrase *liry miloi*—"my dear lyre"—which
uses "lyre" not only as a feminine synonym for "muse," but may
also be interpreted as the "lyre of my beloved."

Perhaps Esenin's feeling that the power of his poetic vision had vanished—"The golden grove has finished speaking / In its merry birch language" (II, 173)—made it easier for him to try adapting his poetry to the political demands of his day. This move constituted a third attempt to reverse his poetic decline.

III   *Political Poems*

On at least two previous occasions Esenin had attempted, with varying degrees of emphasis and success, to strike a "proletarian" Bolshevik note in his poetry, in "The Comrade" of 1917, and in the even more political "Nebesnyi barabanshchik" ("The Heavenly Drummer," 1918). Sensing his own failure, he stopped then, to return to explicitly Communist political themes only in 1924. But his political poems of 1924 were poetically weak. "Ballada o dvadtsati shesti" ("The Ballad of the Twenty-Six," 1924), lacking the touch of his imagery, was but a prosaic retelling of the execution of twenty-six Communist commissars in Baku in 1918. It spoke of the peasantry and proletariat rising together against the Russian empire (II, 180), and associated communism and freedom with the people's rebellion (II, 179). But the perfunctoriness of these statements, devoid of any poetic power, suggested that they did not come from the heart, as the more perceptive of Marxist critics recognized at the time. Esenin had long since committed himself to his envisaged peasant revolution, which had little to do with either communism or the proletariat.

The poem "Stansy" ("Stanzas," 1924) was an even more desperate attempt to come to terms with communism. Esenin even tried to shift some of his symbolic imagery to a Communist plane, as when he wrote that Lenin's name, windlike, activated thought as a wind would move the wings of windmills (II, 192). What gave the poem any conviction at all was in fact certain lines that restated Esenin's poetic dilemma: he felt himself a "step-son" of the USSR, likening his poetic fate to that of an unfortunate, caged canary (II, 192). There was irony in his subdued, humorous remark that he should sit down and do some boring reading in Marx: "Let's get a sniff of the great wisdom / Of boring lines" (II, 193). In view of this emotional background to the poem, it is difficult to believe Esenin's avowal that he was ready to substitute an urban sensibility for the rustic one in his poetry, even when he was full of thoughts about Russia's "industrial power" (II, 194). The ironic final stanza, repeating his self-encouragement to study Marx, did nothing to alleviate the reader's sense of insincerity, or at best incompleteness, in the poem.

Passing praise of Lenin (II, 205) or a fleeting remark that Esenin was a "most passionate fellow traveler" in Soviet Russia (II, 206) could not reverse this impression. And though in "Lenin" (1924) he exalted the Russian leader (see also his "Kapitan zemli" ["Earth's captain," 1925]), Esenin still found the revolutionary world outside unattractive. The old rural way of life haunted his poetic memory. The fact that this poem was left unfinished (the only unfinished piece in Esenin's work) and its sometimes weak and artificial rhyming suggest that Esenin experienced difficulty in composing it.

In "Pesn' o velikom pokhode" ("The Song of the Great Campaign," 1924), as in "Pugachev," the poetic characters and attitudes (the rebellious deacon, the guilt-ridden Peter the Great, the luckless Russian people) spring from Esenin's own psychological state. Whether by coincidence or not, his use of the epic folk meter here goes along with the rebellion motif of his early poetry (cf. "The Song about Evpatiy Kolovrat" of 1912 and "Marfa the Mayoress" of 1914). Yet, if it was Esenin's purpose to write an epic poem of the victorious revolution (see III, 158–59)—that is, to mythologize recent events in ancient folk epic form—he failed, because the fragmented subjectivity of the poem militated against any unifying poetic idea that would have provided the whole a greater objective and historical validity.

The only poetically significant facet of his "Poem About the Thirty-six" (1924) was not its explicit "revolutionary" theme, but the fact that, in thinking of Siberia as a new virgin land, he harked back to his own imagery again: to the "maple" of happier days (III, 167), and to his visionary "bride" motif, where the figure of a girl for a moment personified both spring and his native countryside (III, 168). But the theme of happiness realized was countered by motifs of captivity and vengeance (III, 170, 172). And when, after the revolution of 1917, the revolutionaries

met again, their lives had been normalized: the metaphor of
"putting out the fire in their eyes" suggested the sacrifice
of their ideal vision to life's comforts. In an ironic vein, Esenin
observed:

> Each of them has a new
> House.
> They use them only
> For sleeping quarters,
> Having put out the fire
> In their eyes. (III, 180)

These lines read like the next gradation of disillusionment
after *Tavern Moscow*. The political revolution, he realized, could
be served only at the price of genuine poetry. As a result, in his
poem "Otvet" ("Answer," 1924), outwardly a response to his
mother but actually a veiled, figurative reply to the Soviet
regime, he pitted the power of his own poetic vision of what
he called the "great revolution" against the revolution that had
betrayed him, and now threatened to drain the remainder of his
creative powers. Probably referring to the revolution of 1917
as that "vile blizzard" (II, 216), he exclaimed:

> But that other spring
> Which I love
> I call
> The great revolution.
> I suffer and grieve
> Only for it.
> I wait for and invoke
> Only it. (II, 216–17)

By association, the femine gender of the Russian word "revolution" readily linked the last two lines of the above stanza with
the feminality of Esenin's poetic imagination.

   In view of his failure to produce poetry more consonant with
his political times, it comes as no surprise to find that, side
by side with these poems, Esenin continued to write poetically
more sincere and therefore more resonant poetry, and especially
"Rus' ukhodiashchaia" ("Vanishing *Rus'*," 1924). This was almost

the only poem in which he explicitly protested in his own person against being creatively "muzzled" by communism. Doomed to be "time's manure" (II, 196), he blamed Soviet power for having prevented him from giving full poetic and social expression to himself:

> I blame the Soviet power
> And feel wronged by it
> Because it prevented me from reliving my innocent youth
> In the struggle of others. (II, 196)

He was caught between the old way of life and the new (II, 197); this war-torn time was not conducive to his lyrical poetry, even though he had managed to salvage from the storm lines of unforgettable beauty (II, 196). His poem "Rus' bespriiutnaia" ("Orphan *Rus'*," 1924), written about the thousands of homeless children in Russia at the time, underlined his own homelessness, the outer social confusion signifying his inner poetic perplexity. He confessed in his "Pis'mo k zhenshchine" ("Letter to a Woman," 1924) to an inability to comprehend the meaning and direction of his times (II, 204).

IV   *"Persian Motifs"*

Esenin's strange series of twelve poems entitled "Tsvety" ("Flowers," 1924), which he himself considered "philosophical" and one of his best works, can be taken as marking a poetic reentry into his own world of the imagination after the "political diversion." These poems in a sense anticipated his *Persian Motifs,* where—as he had done in his "Love of a Hooligan" poems—he would once again attempt to revivify his poetic vision through woman.

The cycle of flower poems resuscitated images that had previously been more explicitly connected with his vision of a peasant paradise: for example, the "cornflowers of his beloved's eyes" that were far away, or the "inseparable love" that burned in his heart (II, 220). There was, also, what one might identify as a sudden metaphysical rationalization in the event of poetic failure in Esenin's poems VI and VIII of this cycle, where the allegory of rowanberries born out of the death of their blossoms became a figure for his own poetic growth even if he were never to see his beloved, that is, continued growth even after the "death" of his vision (II, 221–22). But this poetic stoicism, unusual for Esenin, vanished in the sudden reawakening of his poetic spirits in "Vesna" ("Spring," 1924). Of particular note is one stanza that foreshadowed his *Persian Motifs*: a young girl would come to water the maple—which he had just called a "pillory," old and shabby (II, 235)—so that it would be capable of struggling with the snowstorms during "grim October" (II, 239). With this he announced the poetic function of his *Persian Motifs*.

Esenin's *Persian Motifs*, coming immediately after his "Spring" and conceived between the autumn of 1924 and the summer of 1925, were all written in the South, for the most part in the Caucasus. The geographical separation from the centers of power and the traditional poetic attraction of the South no doubt contributed to the resurgence of Esenin's creative inspiration. As had been the case with his "Love of a Hooligan" cycle, the Shagane who inspired the fifteen poems of this cycle actually existed,[3] but the poetic references to her as well as to her legendary sisters—inspired by readings in Omar Khayyam, Sadi, Firdausi, and the *Arabian Nights*—transcended the female figures of his poems, symbolizing a renewed and final attempt to consummate and satisfy, through the figure of woman, his romantic yearning for a paradisal state of being where the wounds suffered during his unequal struggle with the State—and perhaps even with the world in general—could finally heal, and where a turbulent heart could find tranquility.

The very first poem of the *Persian Motifs* suggested that Esenin was willing to "steal" the pleasures promised by his lady-love from her lord and master (III, 8), a metaphorical way, perhaps, of stating that he was prepared to slip by the watchful eye of his times in order to "possess" his ideal vision. "Persia" was now attending to his "past wound" and his "drunken delirium" (III, 7). Having in imagination transported himself to Persia, he could, by a geographical sleight of hand, even reflect upon the poetic regimentation under which he suffered at home: "In Russia we do not keep spring maidens / Chained like dogs" (III, 7). The second poem reiterated the idea that love (for Laila) could only be expressed through stealth and in mute passion (III, 9). The third poem, addressed to the less mythical Shagane, was filled with the old images of his native countryside—springtime, burning eyes, the rye fields of Ryazan in the moonlight. Poetry became a "painkiller," an anesthetic: "I don't feel any pain at all" (III, 11). Still, all was yet not well, for he implored Shagane not to "disturb his memories" of home (III, 12).

Now he could suddenly *see* again through Shagane's eyes: "I have seen the sea in your eyes / Blazing in a light blue fire" (III, 14). Subtly he suggested that Shagane was the incarnation of his bridal vision in the line "Invisible, you called me" (III, 15). But as one reads deeper into the cycle of poems, it becomes all too evident that a poetry of temporary oblivion would not do, that poetic experience could not be suppressed or transplanted, and that, to be organic, it must draw upon its own roots. Thus, for example, using the image of the "veil," Esenin suggested that nature's gifts, the body's natural beauty, should not be concealed (III, 16–17), that the poet in fact should only be himself and never try to block the natural expression of self: "Dear love, don't be friends with the veil" (III, 17). After this disguised reference, perhaps, to his poetic accommodation of the Communist regime, Esenin in the next poem despaired of reaching the end of his poetic journey. He saw himself perishing on the way, with only the illusion of having found peace in Peri's embraces to the playing of Hassan's flute: "Here it is, the wished-for destiny / Of all who have grown tired on the way" (III, 19). Exhausted by his journey, he would not reach his sacred destination: "Wanderer, going off into the azure, / You will not reach the desert cloister" (III, 18). His vision would break; it could not be sustained: "Your gaze will falter" (III, 18), and he would drink in the fragrant wind coming from paradise only with "parched lips" (III, 19). Sheherazade's garden had also stopped echoing her song (III, 20). Only once did Esenin's epoch intervene in his poetry, when he mused rather ironically that "paradise" was much closer at hand and that all it took to regain blissful peace was to surrender to the enemy (III, 20).

His poem "V Khorossane est' takie dveri," ("There are doors

in Khorassan," 1925) returned to the idea of his stealing in to his beloved, though now he found he could not open the doors leading to her chambers (III, 22). Perhaps his poetry was useless, he mused; perhaps it was time to return to his old Russia, i.e., to get back to reality (III, 22). And as he took leave of his lovely Peri, he thanked her for at least allowing him to experience a "beautiful suffering" of which he could sing once he was home again. It is noteworthy that the first and last lines of the poem's final stanza would soon echo through his suicide poem:

> Good bye, Peri, good bye.
> Even though I could not unlock the doors,
> You gave me beautiful love songs,
> With which I can sing of you at home,
> Good bye, Peri, good bye. (III, 23)

That his poetic vision of long ago had not essentially changed at all, and that it still inspired his poetry, is clear from one of the last poems of the cycle, "Ruki miloi—para lebedei—" ("The arms of my sweetheart are a pair of swans," 1925):

> All human beings on this earth
> Sing and repeat the song of love.
>
> I too sang it once upon a time, far away,
> And now once again I sing about the very same things,
> This is why my words full of gentleness
> Breathe so deeply. (III, 28)

However, he concluded that his "song of love" had ruined him: "But the pair of swans has undone me" (III, 29). He was unsure for the moment whether he should follow out his vision to its ineluctable end—"If I drink my soul's love to its very dregs," or "If I burn myself out in dear Shaga's arms" (III, 28) —or live on to a ripe old age, on the memory of his bold poetic feat.

As if in answer, creative nature took its course. He found himself losing his poetic transport: "Why does the moon shine so dully / On the walls and gardens of Khorassan? / It is as if I were walking on the Russian plain" (III, 30). Now even Shagane had betrayed him with another (III, 30). Happiness had deceived him (III, 32); he would abandon his search for paradise (III, 33). The last poem of the cycle—reminiscent of Konstantin Batyushkov's "Podrazhanie drevnim" poems, "In Imitation of the Ancients," written shortly before his mental collapse in 1823—returned to an earlier image in *Persian Motifs,* that of the light blue sea aflame in his love's eyes:

> Light blue, cheerful land.
> My honor has been sold for song.
> Sea wind, blow more gently
> Do you hear how the nightingale calls out for the rose? (III, 34)

He had sacrificed his life to poetry, the end was near, but still, defiantly and desperately, he celebrated the power of his lyrical achievement, rejoiced at having wedded his song to nature, at having let his poetry speak naturally and unaffectedly. This would have to be recompense for his failure to possess his ideal beloved:

> Light blue, cheerful land.
> Even if all my life has been sold for song,
> Yet, instead of Geliya, the nightingale embraces the rose
> Under shadowy branches.   (III, 35)

V   *Poetic Decline*

In the rest of his poems of 1925, Esenin moved ever closer to the final disintegration of his poetic vision. His poem "Moi put'" ("My Path"), notwithstanding the affirmative tone of its last stanza, recorded his concealment of the fact that his poetic inspiration had cooled: "In order not to betray / The cold of my eyes" (III, 47). Now he only imagined that he was actually embracing his beloved (III, 53). Both she and he had ceased flowering (III, 54). Thoughts of poetic impotence and death began to flood his imagination:

> Withering power!
> Well, if I have to die, I'll die!
> To the very end I would like to kiss
> My love's lips.   (III, 56)

Now he could return to his father's house only as "half-corpse, half-skeleton" (III, 57). It was as a result of his poetic condition that, instead of looking to the future, an increasing number of poems like "My Path" began to look *back* to his and his family's past (see "Pis'mo k sestre" ["Letter to My Sister," III, 61–63]; and "Anna Snegina" [III, 182–208]). He admitted that he was ill, and could look forward only as far as his own death. Quoting Pushkin, he seemed to be saying that blessed was the poet who had *not* outlived his poetic power (III, 63). Though his love for Russia caused him to exclaim—not too convincingly—that he wanted to see his poverty-ridden country industrialized (III, 69), his own blood was perishing with cold, and his creative powers were ebbing away (III, 70).

An eerie and highly symbolic poem "Vizhu son. Doroga chernaia" ("I see a dream. A dark road") suddenly spoke of Esenin's two beloveds—his love of yore, and another "beloved," who was like a sleep or a dream coming on a white steed, Death —A beloved comes to me. / . . . / Only she is not loved" (III, 71).

> Oh, Russian birch of mine!
> Narrow and straight path of mine.
> With your branches
> Your arms and hands that do not miss the mark
> Do stop this beloved who is like a sleep
> On behalf of that other one, with whom I'm in love. (III, 71)

Esenin's seeking the birch's protection was itself suggestive of his life-long pursuit of a bridal-paradisal vision. This was the only poem in which poetic vision and its death drew closer to symbolize the creative crossroads he was about to reach. And for the sake of his envisioned Russia, he was willing to drain even the cup of death: "For birch-treed Russia / I will make peace with the one I do not love" (III, 72).

Esenin felt crippled, ready to burn himself out—"If I have to burn, then I'll burn down to the very end" (III, 75). His sense of alienation became more acute even though he still considered himself the poet of the "golden wooden peasant hut" (III, 79). Life was a "deception full of an enchanting yearning" (III, 87). Only she who had fired his vision could help—

> I would like to see a nice and lovely girl now
> Under my window
> So that with her cornflower-blue eyes
> And with new words and feelings
> She could bring peace to my heart and soul—
> But only for me,
> And no one else. (III, 90)

But the thought of her lacked even the reality of his ideal, for this maid had too much of the earthbound village girl about her. Even the rowan tree at home had found its geographical locus and lost all of its transcendental import: "Has our rowan tree finished burning, / Shedding its berries under the pure white window?" (III, 93). His poetic imagery was losing its power.

VI *Winter Poems*

To convey the latter symbolically was perhaps the function of a series of winter poems Esenin composed before his suicide.

The world seemed suddenly empty of images and sounds: "There is neither moon nor dog's barking / In this void far and wide" (III, 99). The snow and frost, though they pleased him, suggested the end of poetic inspiration. His soul was "extinguished" (III, 104). His maple had become deranged; it danced drunkenly in a snowy waste (III, 105). His eyes had withered and his heart grown cold (III, 108). He had finally succumbed to indifference. One poem, which employed previous symbolic imagery, expressed his spiritual desolation with especial poignancy:

> Snowy waste, white moon,
> Our native region is covered with a shroud.
> And birches in white weep in the forests.
> Who found his end here? Who died? Is it not I myself? (III, 112)

In yet another poem he confessed that his eyes had grown cold long ago. The light of the moon not only treatened to put out his eyes, but the line idiomatically suggested that there was actually *no* light left, everything was in darkness: "Svet takoi, khot' vykoli glaza . . ." ("The light is such, you could gouge your eyes out," III, 113).

VII *Love Poems*

A last cycle of love poems, suggestively bearing the syntactically incomplete title "Stikhi o kotoroi" ("Poems of her whom"), is one final attempt to gather up the threads of his poetic vision.

Their love had come to a disillusioning end long ago: "[For, you and I know] that we have finished loving long ago / Each loving someone else" (III, 129). Still, he prayed that his vision of the one whom he would never stop loving might forever remain with him: "Let my heart always dream of May / And of her whom I love eternally" (III, 129). And in a stanza that merged his bridal vision with his dream of paradise, he confessed that his last encounter with woman (Benislavskaya? Tolstaya-Esenina?) was but a means by which to evoke a vision of his ideal love:

> It is not you I love, dear one,
> You are but an echo, a shadow.
> In your face I see another
> Whose eyes are like the spirit of the dove.   (III, 130)

He had found it impossible to live his life without a vision, for, as he put it, even if paradise and hell had not existed, man would have invented them (III, 131). There was no more fire left in him (III, 133); like Don Juan, he accepted death's challenge, ready to pay the price for having been a poet, for having once imagined he might soar forever: "One has to pay for having been free with one's feelings" (III, 135). Now even his birch had become "common currency" (III, 136), and he himself was but a dreamer who had spent his vision in the dark (III, 136).

VIII *"The Black Man"*

In "The Black Man," who had accompanied him, shadowlike, for at least two years before his suicide, Esenin gave ultimate expression to his agony at the frustration and disaster of his life's vision. He was very ill, he confided. The field that in "Inoniia" had held out the promise of creative growth and flowering, that "word-bearing meadow" of his (II, 38), was now empty and desolate, with only the wind whistling over it. Alcohol tore at his brain, stripping it as an autumn wind would bare a grove (III, 209).

In an image reflecting the hallucinatory, deranged state of mind of a man poisoned by drink, the metaphor of what had once been a one-winged windmill trying to take off became his head flapping its ears, like a bird its wings, "too weak to drag the feet at its neck" (III, 209).

The black man then came to sit at his bedside, and would not let him sleep a wink all night. He twanged over him, like a monk over a corpse, and cynically traced the poet's life and work in a "sickening book" (III, 210). He likened his life to that of a "drunkard and crook" (*prokhvost i zabuldyga*, III, 210), filled his heart with heavy dread, and told the poet that the latter had spent his life in a land of the "most abominable thieves and charlatans" (III, 210). He called him an "adventurer" of the best sort and a poet "not of an immense, but a gripping hold" (III, 210). He reminded him that he had called some woman over forty (Duncan) a "dirty little slut and also his love" (III, 211). Wasn't he the poet, the black man recalled, who had claimed that happiness was the "skill of the brain and hands" (III, 211)? He had suffered much because of his "broken and deceitful gestures" (III, 211), but did he not know that deception was the "most difficult of the high arts in the world" (III, 211)?

The poet rebuked his visitor. How dared he plumb the depths of his soul, he asked! what did he, Esenin, care about the life of a scandalous poet? At this point, vision and image again were distorted as the black man's eyes "clouded over with a light blue vomit" (III, 211), as if to tell the poet that he was a swindler and a thief who had "so shamelessly, brazenly robbed somebody" (III, 212).

The night had suddenly turned frosty. The crossroads were still, the poet all alone by a window. The entire plain was covered with soft, brittle lime, in an image suggesting the devastation and waste left in the poet's imagination. Poetic vision was arrested in the shape of trees that, like horsemen, had huddled together in his garden (III, 212). Somewhere the "ominous bird of night" was weeping, and "wooden horsemen" scattered "thuds of hooves" (III, 212).

Again the black man returned, his top hat reminding the reader of Esenin's Imaginist period. Much more tenderly now, he inquired how a scoundrel such as the poet could suffer so "needlessly and stupidly from sleeplessness" (III, 213). But then, in a sudden and cruel travesty of the poet's life-long bridal and paradisal vision, the black man remarked ironically that he could be wrong. After all, the moon had come out. What else could a small world drunk on its slumber need? Perhaps the fat-thighed one would secretly come, and the poet would read her his insipid and lifeless verse. Adding insult to injury, the black man reduced the poet's vision of the ideal cruelly to a sexually and erotically crippling plane by describing him as a long-haired, ugly creature trying to impress a "pimply" schoolgirl with a tale of "other worlds" while he himself ached with lust.

A sudden vision of innocence—the poet as a blue-eyed, golden-haired little peasant boy—flitted by. The poet flung his cane into his "accursed guest's" ugly face, only to find that he had cast it at himself in the mirror and shattered his own image. The young moon had just died (III, 214).

After this, Esenin's suicide poem, written in his own blood, could only confirm his poetic death. Without poetry, life had lost its meaning. There was nothing novel about dying in this world. For that matter, living was not novel any more either, he wrote (III, 138).

During his last period Esenin sought desperately to sustain a poetic vision that, perhaps by force of historical circumstance, came to be expressed—especially after his *Tavern Moscow* poems—more in self-centeredly subjective than socially relevant peasant terms. But given this shift of emphasis, and the ultimate disintegration of the power of his creative imagination, his poetic focus remained essentially the same. There was yet no thematic break of any magnitude in his poetic vision. To say this is simultaneously to affirm that Esenin remained and tried to remain much more whole than his poetic "accommodations" might at first sight suggest.

Esenin's unsuccessful attempt at "impersonating" Pushkin and identifying himself with him, as well as his short-lived stint of political "service," were not just symptomatic of his failing poetic powers: they also proved that as a poet he could not be false to himself, even in decline. He could not suddenly decide to view the world either through another poet's eyes, or with the ideological squint of a Communist functionary. So far as we can judge from his poetry of the time, Esenin seems to have realized the futility of both efforts, and that is to his credit. It was only when his much more organic attempts to resuscitate his poetic vision through woman also failed that the specter of poetic impotence became truly ominous. "The Black Man" was but a symbolic confession that the sacred had been profaned, the ideal vision broken. Thereafter, suicide was the last logical act of a distorted and alienated imagination.

CHAPTER 7

The Metaphysics of Vision

IN speaking of Lev Shestov's literary essays, Sidney Monas
has said that Shestov "was interested in the experience
behind the one the writer writes about."[1] Shestov himself, in the
opening lines of his essay on Anton Chekhov, phrased it this
way: "Tchekhov is dead; therefore we may now speak freely
of him. For to speak of an artist means to disentangle and
reveal the 'tendency' hidden in his works, an operation not
always permissible when the subject is still living."[2]

This approach is relevant to Esenin's poetic work. To say
this is to define the body of his poems in terms of a unifying
force or energy that, at a subliminal level, shaped the very content of his lyrical opus, and gave it that specific texture that
would ultimately be taken to symbolize the poet's deeper
philosophic sense of the world, that "experience behind the one
the writer writes about."

Looking back on the thematics of Esenin's imagery, one per-
ceives that the latter communicated essentially a utopian
vision of a peasant's paradise on earth through images taken
from nature and from the immediate spiritual and physical
experience of the Russian countryside, poetically projected and
"personified" through a kind of "neo-Blokian" feminality of
vision. This—what one might term Esenin's "ideological" thematics expressed at one of the levels of poetic perception—was
equivalent to a dynamic life force moving continuously forward
into future time. But at a deeper level (and one of which
perhaps even Esenin was not fully aware) the dynamic, creative life force of his poetic imagination was countered by
its opposite, a "philosophical" and profoundly existential thematics, a latent, destructive, death force, "dynamic" only in
its potential for creative annihilation.

88

I *Lexical Analysis*[3]

A striking feature of Esenin's poetry was the frequency with which words connected with the theme of "death and decay" occurred throughout his work. Most of these words were expressive of "downward motion," including the various ultimate states of rest reached either naturally or through violence. Words denoting or describing sorrow—weeping, melancholy, yearning, dejection, anguish, sadness—were preponderant. Esenin's universe was brittle, both fragile and fluid, tending toward instability. States of exhaustion were also characteristic of Esenin, as was the process of draining or emptying. An array of suggestive atmospheric colors may be related to the same theme.

Esenin's frequent use of words with falling, reducing, felling, disequilibrizing, and weakening action created an overall effect whose essential tone had much in common with the theme of death and decay.

II *Alienation*

Another aspect of the death syndrome in Esenin's work was the theme of alienation with all its ramifications. Alienation in Esenin began with estrangement and ended in eventual derangement. At the bottom of it lay a basic incapacity for real human communication: even in his "utopian" striving, he used human beings merely as raw material for poetic ends. As such, the process of alienation paralleled the disintegration of his personality: this was a particularly agonizing and desolating form of death.

One of the first expressions of alienation was the pilgrim or beggar motif. A representative instance, especially for his early poetry, is the image of Esenin, a pitiable wanderer turned swallowtail in the steppe, singing with the evening star about God (I, 161). He had already proclaimed that he had come to this earth in order the more quickly to depart from it (I, 119). A decade later, in 1925, he still saw himself as an eternally wandering pilgrim (III, 57); later that year he commented that he was but a passer-by in this world (III, 98).

Deceit and betrayal in love, happiness, and life—in essence

a rejection motif—was common in his poetry. As early as 1911, the river pursued him with laughter, informing him that his sweetheart had abandoned him for another man (I, 66); he had nowhere to lay his head. Without happiness, it was burdensome to live a life that was bitter and poor (I, 86). Unloved, he would be rejected even by her whose name he cherished (I, 200). The poem "Pugachev" (1921) was a lyrical, subjective dramatization of the betrayal-rejection motif. His "Land of Scoundrels" (1922–1923) also spoke in part of betrayal. However, in this case the rejection motif was more positive, since Nomakh himself rejected the society that was bent on eliminating him.

To the end Esenin seems to have felt rejected. In his *Persian Motifs* (1924–1925) he sounded this note again, as the woman he loved lay with another (III, 27). Bitterly he exclaimed that everyone was "deceived by happiness" (III, 32); the world had become deceit and illusion. Once more he discovered he meant nothing to his beloved (III, 91); each day found him with another, because he could not accept the bitterness that came of these many betrayals (III, 134). In this connection, mention might also be made of Esenin's dread of ridicule, especially strong during the final two years of his life (II, 172; III, 134).

It was perhaps indicative of the break in Esenin's personality that the outcast motif should have figured in his poetry from beginning to end. As early as 1911, he was attracted to such themes as those found in "Pesnia starika razboinika" ("The Song of the Old Robber"), in which the old man wistfully remembered how he had once been a cut-throat and robber (I, 81). In "Razboinik" ("The Robber," 1917), for instance, Esenin was himself the highwayman waiting for his prey (I, 299–300). In "The Hooligan" (1920), he admitted that he was by nature a horse thief and bandit (II, 100). Of course, both Pugachev and Nomakh were antisocial individuals. But the most poignant rendering of the outcast motif occurs in the *Tavern Moscow* cycle of poems, where Esenin associated himself with the tavern world of the disillusioned, with its brigands and prostitutes (cf. II, 121–22). As late as 1925 he cried out that he was still a hooligan, that nothing had changed (III, 72). Whether to offset the pain, or whether it was a part of the peasant's psyche, Esenin felt a certain pride in being an outcast of one type or another. In "Anna Snegina," for instance, he declared that in 1917 he had been his country's first deserter (III, 185). And yet there was a melancholy undertone in the lines in which he aligned himself with the homeless: "We are all of us homeless, we don't need much. / I just sing with what has been given me" (III, 101).

Associated with the outcast motif is the theft motif. In Esenin's early poetry, this usually appeared as a seductive intent to carry off a sweetheart (I, 67). In the "Land of Scoundrels," Nomakh saw himself at one point as a kind of Robin Hood (IV, 210–11); later on, in his *Persian Motifs,* Esenin reverted to his role of seducer or abductor of beautiful maidens (III, 8).

Another strong current in Esenin's poetry flows from nature, a source of Esenin's further alienation from humankind. Rejected by society, he sought intimate refuge in nature and the animal kingdom, at the expense of human communication. One thinks in this connection of his poem "Egoriy" of 1914, for instance (I, 100–102). However, from a sympathetic defender of wolves, Esenin could readily transform himself into a shepherd with a great affinity for nature (I, 131). At certain moments in his life, he could display a high degree of empathy with the sufferings and fate of animals, as in his "Song about a Dog" of 1915. In "Mares' Ships" (1919), his sole contacts were dogs and bitches (II, 89). Esenin's wish to be nonhuman could emerge in an intense longing for absolute blending with nature, as in, for example, his desire to stand like a tree near the road (II, 91). He felt at ease in the company of all kinds of animals. Pigs' dirty snouts were to his liking, and the croaking of toads in the silence of the night delighted him (II, 102). In his "Song about Bread" (1921), a poem resembling a dirge to harvesting, he ascribed an animal sense even to grain, when he compared ears of wheat being chopped down by sickles to swans having their necks severed (II, 105).

This same affinity for nature was expressed by Khlopusha in "Pugachev" (IV, 178), and by Pugachev himself, who likened his soul to a small animal tossing and turning in its lair (IV, 171). In "Wolf's End" (1922), Esenin spoke of himself as a wolf at bay; in *Tavern Moscow* he confessed to having no friends among people; he could be friendly only with horses and dogs

(II, 119–20). He knew, he said, how to charm dogs and mares from the steppe (II, 136), and in the haunting "Sobake Kachalova" ("To Kachalov's Dog," 1925), the dog was his confidant (III, 49–50). Finally, in "My Path" (1925), he spoke tenderly of his much-loved birch tree, which in his eyes had always been a substitute for woman (III, 47).

Spiritual revolt—which usually accompanies the birth of a new religion, and which amounts to a quite active rejection of the status quo—can be directly related to the act of alienating oneself from others. The poems Esenin wrote in 1917–1918, while in a state of prophetic, religious, revolutionary fervor—probably the most optimistic of all his works—may serve as good examples of this. Allied to this spiritual revolt with its power to alienate is that "historical," or "political," revolt that was in whole or in part artistically expressed in such early poems as "Marfa the Mayoress" (1914), through "Pugachev" (1921), to the political poems of 1924–1925.

The pose of the religious elect that Esenin assumed in his "Inoniia,"—the prophetic tendency of his vision, though afterwards muted, never vanished from his poetry—was in turn also partly sustained by Esenin's sense of poetic election, by an innate sense of superiority to ordinary man, a sense that colored the whole of his work and set him aside still further from the common run of humanity. Thus in 1912 he had proudly asserted that what others could not do the poet would do freely and easily (I, 82). The poem celebrating his birth on St. John's Eve emphasized that he was not a child of woman, but of nature (I, 84). The poet's life was marked by the fact that destiny had granted him the gift both to caress and to lacerate (II, 131). To one of his lady-loves in the *Persian Motifs,* he said that he was not bound by any commandments, and that since he had been born a poet, he would kiss her like a poet (III, 13). Gratified—but at the same time isolated in his uniqueness—he wrote that "no one / had ever sung his songs" (III, 36).

The theme of alienation was also carried by the escape motif, whether it stood for flight and abandonment, or for a sheer projection of self into the future. In 1915, while the war was raging, he had exclaimed how restless he felt at home, and how he would wish to swoop down, birdlike, on the battlefield

(I, 151); later, in 1922, he considered his own irresolvable dilemma—torn as he was between urban and rural worlds—and thought the only solution might be to become a tramp and leave everything behind (II, 117). In "To the Poets of Georgia" (1924), he envisioned a time when all men would be brothers and all poets friends, an ideal escape into the future from an unsatisfactory present (II, 208–209). In fact, Esenin's life-long paradisal vision may be interpreted in this sense.

The "stranger" motif was akin to that of the outcast. Its currents ran strong in Esenin's poetry. Early in his life he felt the pain that came with estrangement in love (I, 172). In "Wolf's End" (1922), he portrayed himself pursued and persecuted everywhere, like the wolf (II, 112). In "Vozvrashchenie na rodinu" ("Return Home," 1924), he discovered an unfamiliar world: things had changed, people had changed. He no longer recognized his father's house. The old man he met in the street was his grandfather, though at first he did not know him. His grandfather told him that Esenin's sisters had become Komsomol (Communist Youth) members, that the cross had been taken from the church and its icons discarded, and that he now went to pray to trembling poplars standing in the woods (II, 160–61). Esenin did not feel he was a part of this new world. No one knew him any more and yet he could not shake the habits and associations of the past (II, 162). In "Soviet *Rus'*" (1924) he complained again that nobody knew him, and even those who had once known him had now forgotten him. His father's house lay in ashes. Painfully he realized that this new world no longer had any need either of him or his poetry. He accepted this new world and blessed its new generation, but remained a stranger to it, because he could not metamorphose himself into its poetic spokesman (II, 168–71). His poem "Vanishing *Rus'*" (1924), reflected similar moods. Yet, as he indicated in his "Pis'mo dedu" ("Letter to Grandfather," 1924), his grandfather's world was also beyond reach: "No sled / Can bring you here / To me" (II, 231). Esenin re-created this same sense of isolation in "My Path" (III, 47); in a later "winter" poem "Sinii tuman. Snegovoe razdol'e" ("Blue fog. Snowy expanse," 1925); and he spoke ironically of alienation, using folk forms, in his "Skazka o pastushonke Pete, ego komissarstve i korov'em tsarstve" ("The

Fairy Tale about Pete the Shepherd, of how he Became a Commissar and of his Cow Kingdom" 1925).

Esenin was quite consistent: motifs of superfluousness and uselessness were always amply represented in his work, especially in his later years. He had already described his predicament in "Ia poslednii poet derevni' ("I'm the last village poet," 1920). He was envious of the new generation, of the new man (II, 198). He was even useless from his family's point of view, we learn from "Letter from Mother" of 1924. In "The Snowstorm" (1924) he gave full vent to his tormented isolation, his poetic impotence and unfruitfulness, by writing that he should be strung up for disturbing his country's sleep with his hoarse and ailing song (II, 235).

Esenin's spiritual dilemma brought with it a sense of futility, disillusionment, incompleteness, indifference, even cynicism, elements which then no doubt aggravated his alienated condition still further. In one of his *Tavern Moscow* poems he confessed that he had tried to reach for the impossible, to realize an ideal poetic vision on earth, but that he had failed, and in the process been corrupted:

> I wanted to wed
> The white rose with the black toad.
> Even if these desires going back to my rose-colored days
> Have got out of hand and have not been realized,
> Still, if devils nested in the soul,
> Angels must have lived in it.(II, 131–32)

No assistance seemed in sight in his last years. Even as he desperately sought inner balance and peace, an oppressive anxiety and gnawing illness remained within. All his imaginary "Persian" voyage could give him was "beautiful suffering" (III, 23); it did not provide a cure. Where could he find refuge? Life had become a burden (III, 89–90), a nightmare (III, 124), thoughts of childhood ineffectual (III, 93–94), delirium and madness the only exits left to him.

As early as 1916, notes of delirium had begun to make their appearance in his poetry. Such was the image of stars bathed in invisible madness, which filled a willow tree that had just waked up with fright and terror (I, 209). In one instance in *Tavern Moscow*, contamination, plague and frenzy are associated with love (II, 127). In a poem of 1924, he recorded a delirious experience he had undergone while in a clinic recuperating from a cut wrist. He had imagined he was urging on a troika in the dead of winter; instead he woke up to find himself beating his moist and bloody bandage against the bed (II, 154). Even poetry at times became so insupportable as to resemble a sharp pain in his temples (III, 53), an occurrence that reminds one of the opening lines of "The Black Man":

> Friend,
> I am ill, very ill, my friend.
> I don't know myself where this pain has come from.
> At times it seems as if wind whistles over
> An empty and desolate field,
> At others like a wind stripping a grove in September.
> Alcohol tears at my brain, and it falls.   (III, 209)

Alienation brings up yet another aspect of Esenin's poetry: the otherworldly motif, and motifs associated with it. When this motif is involved, Esenin kept shifting his otherworldly focus from this world to the "other," and back again. In schematic terms, a road, distance, expanse, vastness, space pointed to another world, while that other world in turn cast its protean spells on this one. In its most obvious form, the otherworldly motif bore religious, Christian, or other connotations. The voyage, departure, the miracle, transfiguration, each became a poetic ritual, symbolic of Esenin's religious, paradisal quest.

It is not very difficult to discover the mystic sense of another reality or existence in Esenin's early poetry: birches in the moonlight, for example, stood like candles in the night (I, 55). A great number of poems, we recall, bore the otherworldly motif, whether in the form of religious pilgrims, popular saints, or the people's Christ walking the Russian earth. In other poems (such as "Isus mladenets" ["The Infant Jesus," 1916]) there was a constant communication and traffic between the Mother of God and earth's wild creatures. In "The clouds from the place where mares give birth" of 1916, to take another

instance, the other world was transferred to this one in an
almost apocalyptic vision of a new Elysium (I, 249–50).

Esenin went on dreaming about otherworldly glades (I, 256);
the other world was calling, God existed (I, 270). In "Church
Octet for Voice" (1917), he wrote of the establishment of God's
Kingdom on earth and visualized a peasant world become a
final anchoring place for the mythical death ships (I, 281–82).
By the light of that other world, under God's aegis, Esenin was
fated, at the end of time and in resurrected form, to set out on
a voyage to the other world: "But he who conceived in the name
of the Virgin / Shall embark on a starship" (I, 284). In his poem
"O Rus' vzmakhni krylami" ("Oh Russia, try your wings," 1917),
the whole rural world of Russia took off for the other world
(I, 292). "Inoniia" betrayed its "otherworldliness" in the very
title. In a very Blokian vein, Esenin noted that his soul "yearns
for heaven. / It is a native of unearthly meadows." (II, 86).

Distance motifs were associated with this otherworldly focus
and mood. In 1910 grey clouds in deep yearning had already
set sail to a distant land (I, 57). Throughout his work Esenin
expressed his acute sensitivity to space and expanse by dwelling
on fields, meadows, plains, groves, stars, distances, infinite
stretches where only the blue of the heavens sucked at the eyes,
the empty desolation of Russian winter in the country, lakes,
backwoods, streams, the misty and fog-ridden beyond, infinite
vistas, shorelessness. In "Pugachev," the road that had exhausted him led into a terrifying void, however (IV, 159); and
in Esenin's last year of life, he lovingly cursed the discomfiting,
thin mooniness and boring desolation of endless plains (III,
68), or wanted to lose himself in the snowy wastes of a field
(III, 105). One might add in this connection that magic dreams,
fairy tale atmospheres laden with mystery, supernatural forces,
charmed worlds and sorcery are all variations on a theme.

Another symptom of alienation—and part of the death syndrome—was the cold motif. In one of his earliest poems, a snowstorm raged through a courtyard: orphaned sparrows, pressing
themselves against the window pane, related by their orphaned
state to the cold outside (I, 57–58). Snows could bring joy to the
earth (I, 278), but they could also inflict pain and destruction
(II, 47). Still, Esenin confessed that he could not live without

snowstorms (II, 118). It is of some biographical significance that cold motifs began to predominate at the end of his life. His winter poems, with their crisp lucidity, could not have expressed the theme of coldness better. In a poem of 1925 evoking burial associations, he was one with the snowstorm, and fearlessly watched the latter nail his worthless heart, like a white nail, into the roof of a house (III, 111).

In one of Esenin's most haunting poems, the cold motif became associated with the bleak autumnal landscape: valleys had turned light blue in the transparent cold; the sound of hoof-beats was clear and distinct; evening, overhanging the river washed the toes of its blue feet in the white water; his hopes looked bright in the autumnal cold, and his steed ambled along, still as fate (I, 224). He rejoiced in a wind-stilled cry he heard, blowing over a thicket in a dense forest, commenting that he should be as cold as lindens' autumn gold (II, 64).

By association, night, and especially the moon, carried similar connotations. The moon was linked with the North (III, 11). And, in a strange inversion, because Esenin could not do without cold he was warmed by the coolness of the new moon (III, 98). A little later, however, such a winter's cold descended upon the world that even the chill moon was shivering (III, 101). In a poem where he reminisced about a moonlit night of his handsome youth, the realization that his heart had grown cold evoked thoughts of the moon: "My heart has grown cold and my eyes have lost their color. / Blue happiness. Moonlit nights!" (III, 108).

It was no secret to Esenin that he harbored a fatal cold within him. He must have been aware of it long before his indirect admission of 1918, in the poem "Vision" (II, 34). It distorted his view of the external world to the point where even a street lantern reflected in a dark puddle of water seemed chilled to the marrow. To avoid seeing worse things, as he put it, he decided to squint at the world so as to see less of it, for things were a bit warmer and less painful that way (II, 107). In "Flowers," he confessed to the flowers that not just anyone could have discovered that his heart had become chill with cold (II, 220).

In desperation he sought warmth, but to no avail. The stars' fire in the heavenly wastes that chilled his soul gave him no warmth (III, 88). Through a whirling snowstorm he spied a light in the window of his village home (III, 101). In another poem he asked his sweetheart to light a fire in the stove and make the bed for the night; for without her, the snowstorm within him would rage on without end (III, 106).

III *Death*

The theme of death is one of the most pervasive motifs in Esenin's poetry. Death abounded in Esenin's work in all its forms: natural death (I, 59; I, 79) and the wake (I, 170); death in battle (I, 103; I, 112), especially powerfully depicted in "Cossack Us," where a young Cossack wedded his death in the form of a blue snowstorm, and at the wedding feast his beautiful wife became drunk on the red-juiced wines wrung from his mighty frame (I, 115); death by suicide, usually drowning (I, 117; I, 153); murder (I, 235); death by destruction, execution, and violence as in "Lenin" (1924) or "Anna Snegina" (1925).

The imagery of doom and death recurred throughout his poetry, whether in the form of ravens croaking the doom of Russia (I, 145) or as a swift swarm of butterflies anxiously flying at a star (II, 77). Occasionally it was the wind, howling and moaning as if scenting an approaching funeral (II, 234).

Common associated motifs were the motif of the past, as some-thing dear that has vanished (II, 234; III, 20) whether it be the loss of childhood (II, 129; II, 144); youth (I, 72; I, 118; and especially in "Anna Snegina" of 1925 [III, 194, 203, 208]); vigor (I, 204–205; III, 92); dreams and ideals (II, 156; in Nomakh it became disillusionment; IV, 247–49); and past memories of a life with all its familiar associations, never to return (II, 139–40; II, 156; III, 103). When he was not thinking of himself, he reflected on prerevolutionary Russia (IV, 230–31), its poverty-ridden social history (IV, 219–20); and even when he wrote about Lenin, it was in the past tense (III, 142–43).

Closely allied to the past motif was Esenin's acute sense of the passage of time. In the human sense, this was death in process, and autumn with its rain and falling leaves seemed to become its metaphor (I, 75; I, 183). Years dropped into oblivion (I, 206); time was a winged mill (II, 22). The passage of time was especially evident in "Anna Snegina," and in his last year of life he asked his poems to "recount his life quietly" (III, 42). The recurring silence motif was almost a mood accompaniment, a setting for a retrospective view (I, 77; I, 85). Background silence prevailed in the *Persian Motifs*, for instance, and was emphasized by sounds of whispering, fluting, rustling, and by the transparent ethereality of moonlit nights touched by light, fragrant winds (III, 18–19; III, 20–21).

By far the most pronounced expression of the death motif in Esenin occurred in lines revolving about his own death: thoughts of suicide and death, premonitions of personal doom, suggestive parting and absence motifs, a desire for the losing of self, a yielding to self-extinction, a seeking of oblivion. Associated motifs were those of impotence, lack of desire, and resignation, the realization that poetry was a fatal poison bringing with itself frustration and deathly fatigue. In this process he succumbed to the ever-growing power of death, first as a sorceress and finally as that other "beloved" (III, 71–72), the one he had no love for, but who by now alone could pacify his turbulent heart.

Esenin had threatened suicide as early as 1911 (I, 66). In 1915, he exclaimed that he knew only too well that he would soon be buried to the sounds of funeral chants (I, 156). Death as a sorceress, whom even nature feared, whirled with the snow-storm and loomed near (I, 169). In another instance he saw himself returning home to the village: on a green evening outside his window he would hang himself on his own sleeve; he would be buried unwashed, his only mourners grey willows and barking dogs (I, 200–201). He sensed death sharpening her razor in the dark (I, 208). Burning desires aggravated his sick soul, and he envisaged the *kvas* (a fermented drink) and thick gruel of the wake being placed on his coffin (I, 219). Realizing that the mysteries of death were unknowable, he prayed to an icon to "teach him . . . never to waken again" (I, 256).

In the early mornings he loved to lose himself in the east like a star (II, 20). In 1918 he was haunted by thoughts of poetic impotence (II, 63, 76). He yearned to exist in an inert, quiescent state of nondesire, in a nonhuman condition, as when he visualized himself as the moon's face, munching hay and smiling happily at the haystack (II, 18). The moon's wooden timepiece would soon tell his twelfth hour with a rasping sound (II, 97). In a moment of self-realization, he realized that only death could close eyes that had begun to see (II, 108). In his poem from the "Love of a Hooligan" cycle where evening had knit its dark brows, he was a sick man, and death in the form of troika coursers stood outside the gate waiting for someone, waiting to whirl him away into oblivion so that he would no longer recall the somber forces that had preyed on him as they destroyed him (II, 145). Perhaps soon, he wrote in 1924, he would have to collect his transitory belongings for the journey from which there was no return (II, 157). Poetry seemed a fatal poison (II, 202), and he was lost beyond recall; even the moon seemed closer to him than the place where he had been forsaken (II, 225).

In "The Snowstorm" (1924), in a passage drawn from folklore, he imagined that the cat was giving him the fico, as was his mother, transformed into a witch on Kiev mountain. His thoughts came and went helter-skelter, and his ears reverberated with the thuds of burial shovels and the distant sobbing of bell towers (II, 236–37). In his strange poem "To Kachalov's Dog" of 1925, the dog became an intermediary for Esenin's curious act of communion with death (III, 50). He saw death coming for him on a white steed, approaching inexorably along a dark road (III, 71). The moon seemed to be urging him toward suicide (III, 83).

IV *Decay*

Death results in ultimate putrescence, and the decay motif found throughout Esenin's work expresses the poet's disintegration. The theme of decay was carried by the motif of withering. This included the fading of youth and beauty, and the autumnal wizening of nature's features (I, 81; I, 129; I, 161). He liked to convey withering by likening eyes to grains that had spilled and faded (I, 204); he himself was touched by the gold of withering and would never again be young. The flower motif in his work was also connected with wilting and fading. At one point in 1925 he associated flowers with his own death as they bade him a last farewell (III, 118).

Occasionally he spoke of the soul (II, 116), time (II, 166), and life (III, 53) as fading. Occasionally, also, his poetry revealed festering sores in putrid imagery: his decayed corpse (II, 35); an alder tree, its yellow brains trickling out of its head, begging at the roadside (IV, 183); or the moon's horse skull dripping with the gold of rotted spittle (IV, 184). He talked of fat white worms in herrings (IV, 200), and of hapless, superfluous people whose blood was covered with mold, spreading the stench of decay (II, 197).

Esenin ultimately found nothing to fall back upon. Lines he had written to Klyuev in 1918 in which he described the latter as one who had sung his heart out to the Russian *izba* (peasant hut), but who had failed to build a house in his own heart (II, 76) could with equal, if not greater, justice be applied to Esenin. Pugachev, at the moment of his undoing, had asked himself whether one fell under the weight of one's soul as one would under a heavy burden (IV, 196). And Esenin lived out the truth of that insight: death as the dominant mode, as a tragic disease and organic progression, could not be stopped save by its own hand.

CHAPTER 8

Interpretation (1917–1927): Introduction

I Symbolism and Marxism in Russia

IN the poetic development which began in the last decade of the nineteenth century and spanned roughly the first quarter of the twentieth century in pre- and postrevolutionary Russia, there existed a theoretical interdependence of poetic movements, a tacit agreement on the Romantic conception of the nature of the creative process—usually vociferously denied by each succeeding literary group—that engendered a marked continuity in creative sensibility, if not in actual method of composition. Hence such movements as Acmeism, Futurism, and Imaginism owe much more to Russian Symbolist poetic experience than to the tradition of nineteenth-century Realism. The specific spiritual continuum in which these movements worked sustained its creative momentum into the 1920s, despite the disruption caused by the Bolshevik revolution of 1917, which had its own ideas on cultural renascence.

The word "disruption" should perhaps be qualified. The revolution of 1917, even if politically justifiable, disturbed, perhaps not so much the moral as the existing *artistic* lines of force, in the sense that its dominance of art and literature was due not so much to a natural creative process as to historical and political circumstance. Without political backing, Marxist literary theory would never have played the decisive role in matters of art that it eventually did.

Both Marxist and Symbolist movements had been a part of prerevolutionary social and cultural reality. Marxism as a viable political force and Symbolism as a new sensibility had both taken their active beginnings in the 1890s and were—apart from

102

their connection with intellectual and artistic trends in Western Europe—if not direct outgrowths, then in some fashion connected with nineteenth century Russian cultural developments. Marxism, as a humanitarian doctrine for transforming society, could easily draw upon the "radical" Realism, or "materialist" tradition of thought, inaugurated by the critic Vissarion Belinsky in the first half of the nineteenth century. Russian Symbolism, on the other hand, as a spiritual and aesthetic movement was the natural climax of the Russian Romantic spirit of the nineteenth century, a poetic experience whose transcendental visions had already been partially glimpsed by such Romantic poets as Mikhail Lermontov and Fedor Tyutchev.

Thus rooted and coexisting in prerevolutionary Russia, both movements shared—at least in theory—a central concern with the creative liberation of man as a corollary to the cultural significance of human freedom. Alexander Blok's vision of a new "artist-man" (*chelovek-artist*)[1] who would transform the moral fiber and creative potential of men and women in society is not radically different in conception from Marx's utopian "classless man" of the future. But beyond this central concern, both movements reflected in their own way the moral and intellectual searching, the cultural questionings that had characterized the Russian intelligentsia ever since its inception at the end of the eighteenth century. The spiritual search for self, for identity, for national meaning, for that sense of uniqueness that would set Russia apart from the rest of Europe, coupled with the moral longing of generations of educated Russians to reform, or, if worst came to worst, to remake Russian society, to throw off a spiritually encumbering despotism—all this movement toward national and cultural self-awareness found resonance in both Marxism and Symbolism. In fact, to use an apt phrase from Edgar Allan Poe, that "overacuteness of the senses" characteristic of the Russian Symbolists symptomized a final emotional exertion that—in the symbolic desperation of its images and the creative frustration attendant upon such excessive or obsessive flights of soul—capped the spiritual strain of a century of self-seeking. And what Symbolism failed to achieve socially or politically was left to a kindred Marxian spirit to realize. In this sense, the revolution of 1917 seemed, at least at the time, to fulfill the spiritual aspirations of a whole line of Russian thinkers, writers, and poets.

II *The Symbolist Legacy*

Although the decline of the Symbolist movement in Russia is usually dated from 1910, Symbolism proved its creative vitality by successfully generating new schools of poetry. Such movements as Acmeism, Futurism, and Imaginism shared with Symbolist poetic sensibility a poetic intensity of experience, a conviction that poetry was something sacred, omnipotent, set above both men and their gods. This explained their profound concern with imagery, rhythm, and poetic sound as the earthly pulsations of unbound and autonomous forces of creation. Consequently, in their view poetry not only reflected a private glimpse of a usually unacceptable social existence, but was itself a higher and universal vision capable of redeeming, even if for brief moments, the poet's—man's—ontological sense of duality, earthly insecurity, emotional alienation, the failures and frustrations of the everyday world. In this way these poetic movements shared a tragic sense of life opposed to the optimism of Marxist doctrine. Hence, the emotional nature of the aesthetic impulse in these movements, the belief in the spiritual dimensions of metaphor, even their egocentric, almost desperate, iconoclasm cannot be fully understood without some reference to the age of Russian Symbolism.

When the Acmeist, Futurist, and Imaginist poetic impulses spilled over into the postrevolutionary era, they did so, in a sense, as carriers of Symbolist feeling and influence. But at the same time they remained loyal to their own prerevolutionary aesthetic incentives and methods of craftsmanship. Such methods, in the case of Russian Futurism, had tenuous links not only with Filippo Marinetti's Italian Futurist movement, but were also intimately connected with Russian Expressionist painting of the time (e.g., Kazimir Malevich, Natalia Goncharova, Vasily Kandinsky, and Vladimir Burlyuk). But Vladimir Mayakovsky's post-1917 Futurism cannot really be viewed in proper spiritual and poetic perspective independently of his prerevolutionary longer poems. The Acmeists, Nikolay Gumilev and Anna Akhmatova, also remained true to themselves and their art in revolutionary Russia. Even Blok's revolutionary poem *Dvenadtsat'* (*The Twelve*) loses in meaning to the degree that it is removed from the stream of his poetry before the revolution. The Imaginists (whose prerevolutionary impulse also came from English Imagism) cannot be fully appreciated without an understanding of the aesthetic impetus of Nikolay Klyuev's, Sergey Gorodetsky's, and Sergey Esenin's pre-1917 poetry.

Nor is this interpenetration of poetic assumptions, values, and ideas surprising if one recalls the poetic flux that existed before and to some extent after the revolution. Thus members of one group could convert to another, or else acknowledge their Symbolist descent. Thus in 1924 the Acmeist Osip Mandelshtam observed that all of contemporary Russian poetry had come out of the Symbolist family womb (*vyshla iz rodovogo simvolicheskogo lona*).[2] The Acmeist Gorodetsky aligned himself with a peasant-oriented poetic group during the war; it was no doubt the easier for him to do so because, prior to his involvement with Acmeism, he had written poems celebrating a mythical, ancient Russia, with its world of nature and people sentimentalized. At the time of the revolution, the Symbolists Andrey Bely and Alexander Blok joined the Imaginist Esenin on the pages of Ivanov-Razumnik's journal *The Scythians*. The Futurist Vadim Shershenevich joined the Imaginists. An Imaginist volume published in 1919 included among its contributors Bely and Esenin, the Futurist Vasily Kamensky, Boris Pasternak, the peasant poet Petr Oreshin, and the Imaginist Anatoly Mariengof.[3]

The reality of a continuing interdependence or interaction between prerevolutionary groups of poets is equally valid for such proletarian-oriented post-1917 poetic movements as *The Smithy*. This group cannot be properly appreciated without some knowledge of its organic links with the past, i.e., without an awareness of the Symbolists' intuitive, cosmic, almost mystic feeling for existence; the "Adamism," the moral manliness of the Acmeists; and the idealization of urban consciousness by the Futurists in prerevolutionary times. The "Serapion Brothers" learned more from Evgeny Zamyatin and Maxim Gorky than they did from Marxist literary theory and practice. And Kon-

stantin Fedin's novel *Goroda i gody* (*Cities and Years*) and
Yury Olesha's *Zavist'* (*Envy*) owe more to Bely's novel *Peterburg*
(*St. Petersburg*) than they do to the contemporary "proletarian"
novels of the day.

III   *The Cultural and Literary Dilemma of the 1920s*

Between the communist military stabilization signaled by the
end of the civil war (1921) and the political consolidation of
the Stalinist dictatorship begun in 1928, lay the so-called NEP
period, that of the New Economic Policy, a temporary Marxist
compromise and retrenchment on the economic and agricultural
fronts. With the regime's attention fixed primarily on the bread
and butter issues of ruling a state, the 1920s became a time
of cultural stabilization. Even today in the Soviet Union, that
era evokes memories of a lost golden age, a time of relative
creative freedom, experimentation, and genuine artistic achievement. It was a period when various artistic streams and orienta-
tions were still tolerated, and could vie creatively with one
another.

But the coexistence of differing artistic and literary trends
was itself a manifestation of Soviet Russia's cultural dilemma.
After the civil war and a large exodus of the Russian intelligentsia
had created something of a cultural vacuum, the Soviet government—cf. its resolution of June 1925 on the literary situation—
could not wholeheartedly support extreme demands for proletarian predominance in art and literature without thereby com-
mitting cultural suicide. It is probably no coincidence that
Marxist critics and intellectuals highly placed within the government apparatus (such as Anatoly Lunacharsky, the commissar
of education, or Lev Trotsky, commissar of foreign affairs)
spoke out in favor of absorbing the cultural heritage of the
past into the texture of Soviet society. The official intent was
quite clearly to shore up the cultural front at home by winning
over to the Soviet side as many uncommitted or vacillating
artists, writers, and poets as possible.

It developed that a fundamental obstacle to the fulfillment
of this intent was what one might term the Romantic legacy
in art of creative freedom as the prime prerequisite for spiritual

and cultural expression. The Communist attempt to elaborate its own aesthetic based on a fusion of the Marxist concept of economic and social determinism with the party's utilitarian ethic of political service was from the outset doomed to failure, since the notion of a "social command" negated in practice the creative freedom necessary to the artist. As the Stalinist period showed only too well, prescriptive literary service in its Socialist Realist guise to a political cause could only be accomplished at the expense of artistic freedom, integrity, and worth.

The failure to found an operative Marxist aesthetics in the twenties, apart from motives of state, further explains not only the official tolerance of politically neutral literary movements in the face of a mounting Marxist critical offensive, but also strongly suggests the viability of the Romantic spirit.

The "aesthetic" struggle between Marxists and non-Marxists (or Fellow Travelers as they were called) divided artists and writers. What separated the two camps—their subdivisions aside— was their view of priorities in literary criticism. For the Fellow Travelers, art remained the primary consideration, even when some of them—like Mayakovsky and Valery Bryusov—at least outwardly seemed to pass within the Marxist periphery. In their emphases and sensibilities, the Fellow Travelers were the heirs of the prerevolutionary Romantics and Symbolists. The ultimate critical motivation for the Marxists was political commitment, even though some of them, like Alexander Voronsky, tried to reach an artistic *rapprochement* with the Fellow Travelers.

But the "aesthetic" controversy signified a cultural struggle, and was symptomatic of a search for a new and revolutionary culture, a quest that stirred the imagination of contemporaries generally. The cultural debate became a second intellectual issue (after the artistic one) with which all poets and writers had to deal. Polemically formulated, the quarrel centered around the question of whether it was possible to create immediately a proletarian Communist culture without drawing at all upon the Russian and European cultural heritage of the past.

This issue was so divisive that it even split the Marxists among themselves. There were critics—Trotsky and Voronsky— who refused even to contemplate the notion of a rapid creation

of a proletarian culture in a vacuum, and who therefore argued
for the preservation of cultural links with the past. Others—
Lunacharsky and Georgy Yakubovsky—while in essential agreement with the latter view, nonetheless believed in the eventual
triumph of proletarian culture (as distinguished from the classless socialist society prophesied by Marx). The more militant
and pragmatic critics, like G. Lelevich (pseudonym of Labori
Gilelevich Kalmanson), however, thought that the political success of the revolution augured well for the imminent appearance
of an exclusively proletarian culture, and consequently that
this justified the literary and cultural existence of only proletarian-oriented groups. Excessively optimistic and zealous, they
either downgraded or totally rejected the cultural achievements
of the past.

The Marxist cultural positions—in theory at least, if not always
in actual literary critical practice—naturally colored critical attitudes toward the Fellow Travelers, those living links to the
past. The most militant proletarian critics denied the Fellow
Travelers any significant cultural role in contemporary Soviet
society. Among other Marxist critics, toleration of Fellow
Travelers varied as the distance separating them from their
most militant colleagues increased. The Fellow Travelers, both
critics and writers (Esenin included), were naturally at odds
with the Marxists to the degree that the latter begrudged them
the right to creative and cultural coexistence.

IV   *Two Epochs in Collision*

The tensions of the literary and cultural milieu created difficult
conditions for a Fellow Traveler like Esenin: the pressures of
a revolutionary world in search of itself harassed the poetic
imagination intent upon creative survival.

And survival was literally at stake. The critical battle waged
over Esenin and his poetry was, indeed, a contest between two
opposing forces, two eras, two conceptions of reality: Romanticism and revolutionary pragmatism, the prerevolutionary ideal-
ism of a Symbolist age and the materialism of a world in
upheaval, one seeing the infinite potential of man only in his
free individuality, the other believing that only collective and

regimented man could advance historically. The confrontation involved two mutually exclusive assumptions as to the nature of the creative imagination; one camp defended the right of the Romantic poet to pursue the unpredictable poetic flashes of his creative subconscious; the other espoused a prescriptive revolutionary conception of the poet's utilitarian function in society. One thinks of Valeryan Pravdukhin's observation that Esenin's inner rebellion against the "inanimate mechanism of civilization"[4] exposed one epoch's fear of another. In that unequal struggle, Esenin perished. But his very defeat simultaneously represented the triumph of his poetic individuality, which he had vowed never to relinquish except to the power of genuine song.

CHAPTER 9

Fellow Travelers

I *The Scythians: Esenin and Ivanov-Razumnik*

ALTHOUGH *The Scythians* appeared only twice between 1917 and the end of 1918, Ivanov-Razumnik's publication was the first "revolutionary" journal to attract Esenin to its pages. To be sure, Esenin refused to participate in a third issue (which never materialized anyway), but that was because he was poetically offended by Ivanov-Razumnik's praise of Klyuev as "Russia's first profound poet of the people," and not because he wished to break with Ivanov-Razumnik, whom he had known before the revolution. As late as March of 1922 he wrote Ivanov-Razumnik that he was looking forward to contributing to a forthcoming journal of his, and that it was high time to become one family again.[1]

Admittedly, that same letter betrayed Esenin's disenchantment with the Imaginists, whom he had joined in 1919. But it also shows that over a period of some four years after the revolution, Esenin kept in touch with Ivanov-Razumnik (six letters to him have been published), and that, shortly before his trip abroad, Esenin would have welcomed the opportunity to collaborate with him once again.

What attracted Esenin to the Scythians in the first place? Undoubtedly Ivanov-Razumnik's personality had exerted a powerful influence on him from the outset. Possibly he was drawn even to the group's very name, which evoked historic associations with an ancient past when Scythian barbarians had overrun the "Russian" land and left impressive artistic achievements to posterity. Psychologically, the ancient ring of the name *Skify*—which in Russian still retains a primitiveness, a certain austere and wild vigor—would especially have appealed to

110

Esenin: it gave him a sense of the barbarian he was without causing him to forfeit his artistic sensibility.

The Scythians was oriented toward socialism, but Ivanov-Razumnik was highly critical of Marxist economic determinism because, in his view, it stunted individual spiritual and ethical initiative. Without such initiative, man, he believed, could not pass through the cleansing fires of socialism to arrive at future liberation.[2]

It is this spiritually purifying kind of socialism that Ivanov-Razumnik saw at work in the revolution of 1917. At a much later date, as an exile in the West (1942–1943), he remarked that the Scythians—among whom he included Bely, Blok, Klyuev, and Esenin—had stood for a " 'deepening' of the political revolution into a social one."[3] The fires of Scythianism (*skifstvo*), or spiritual maximalism, that Ivanov-Razumnik found burning in the revolutionary upheaval as a promise of man's final liberation, bore a direct relation both to his conception of the development of nineteenth century literature as the gradual emancipation of Russian creative individuality from an oppressive philistinism,[4] and his notion that in a very essential way his socialism was a spiritual continuation of the original religious impulse of Christianity.[5]

No doubt the idea of a spiritual religious movement in the tradition of the Russian intelligentsia, with its dreams of individual and collective liberty, must have struck a sympathetic chord in Esenin's peasant mentality. But even more than that, Ivanov-Razumnik's belief that the Russian soul carried within itself a potential for spiritual maximalism, and that the gifted poet could give it expression in his work and thus become the national spokesman of a movement destined to liberate and save Russia and all Europe, certainly must have fired Esenin's poetic imagination. His chauvinism, as well as the poetic vanity of one who wished to be counted among those poets who, according to Ivanov-Razumnik, had been such national spokesmen (Alexander Pushkin, Fedor Tyutchev, Vladimir Solovev, and Alexander Blok), did the rest.[6]

Hence, when Ivanov-Razumnik interpreted Blok's two revolutionary poems (*The Twelve* and "The Scythians") as expressions of the spiritual revolt accompanying the revolutionary ferment of 1917 and prophesying the future liberation of man,[7] he equated poetic power with the morally transforming force of Scythianism.[8]

Ivanov-Razumnik saw Esenin's "revolutionary" poetry in the same light. He wrote that Esenin, in his elemental poetic affinity for the revolution, was indeed a genuine spokesman of the Russian people at large, and that he expressed that "profound power of the earth" destined for future victory.[9] Ivanov-Razumnik held to this belief as late as 1923.[10]

In discussing Esenin's poems "Otherworldly Call," "Church Octet for Voice," and "The Coming," written in 1917, Ivanov-Razumnik saw Esenin not only as identified with the people, but the people themselves as spiritually reborn in the revolution through his poetry. And Jesus's renewed self-sacrifice—in Esenin's poem "The Comrade" (1917)—for the revolution and in the name of the suffering Russian people became to Ivanov-Razumnik a symbol of God's spiritual triumph in history, insuring man's future freedom.[11]

As for Esenin's "Inoniia" (1918), Ivanov-Razumnik saw it as an attack on historical Christianity, but he viewed its blasphemies as the underside of a God seeking that would bear all the more fruit since, for Ivanov-Razumnik, Esenin was a poet not of erudition, but of intuition.[12]

In an article of 1925, Ivanov-Razumnik called Esenin the last major poet of the golden age, by which he meant the poetic period preceding 1917. He considered Esenin unsurpassed in the contemporary silver age of epigones, who lacked spiritual and creative fire and whose works no longer displayed that cultural (read Symbolist) focus that had been the product of an integral world view.[13]

In retrospect, one may wonder whether Esenin's "religiousness," motivated, as Esenin himself admitted, by poetic and creative considerations,[14] could have had any place in Ivanov-Razumnik's Christian-oriented socialism; and whether in fact the universality that Ivanov-Razumnik ascribed to the revolution was reflected in Esenin's poems of 1917–1918, poems which, if anything, expressed a peasant's chauvinistic anti-Western bias (compare the third part of "Inoniia"). The revolution served Esenin more as a source of poetic inspiration and material than as a spring of revolutionary socialism destined to reform the world. Altruism was, in any case, something of a rarity in Esenin's character.

II *Esenin and the Imaginists*

To Esenin poetry—and poetic imagery in particular—had always been a spiritual extension of the self into an otherworldly dimension of being, a means of escape from a profound human alienation and his personal dilemma, a search for personal completion and liberation. His poetry never lost that sense of otherworldliness, that "religious" or mystic sensibility, so evident in his prerevolutionary poems.[15]

This particular poetic vision most probably brought Esenin to the Scythians in the first place. He joined them precisely because Ivanov-Razumnik's belief in the spiritual function of poetry, his faith that art had the power to reach out beyond itself, supported his own poetic theory and practice.

Esenin's idealistic "Kliuchi Marii" ("The Keys of the Soul") written in 1918 shortly before he joined the Imaginists, sheds light on his poetic orientation at a time when he was gravitating both toward a Scythian populism and an Imaginist aestheticism.

The Russian peasant's "future victory," prophesied by Ivanov-Razumnik and supporting Esenin's vision of a peasant utopia, was one axis along which Esenin's thought in "The Keys of the Soul" developed. The Russian ploughman, he wrote, would soon communicate with God from an earth that was all his own. He envisaged a peasant paradise on earth, a peasant socialism, a free people enjoying a plenteous way of life in which the lost harmony between nature and the essence of man had been recovered.[16]

From this followed Esenin's rejection of Marxist spiritual prescription. Hostile to proletarian guidance in matters of art,[17] he opposed Marxist restrictions upon the artist's creative freedom because it was impossible to channel the complexity of the human soul within the prescribed range of one specific "melody or sonata."[18] Creative freedom thus had a peasant dream as its corollary; and both were fused in a poetic intuition and spiritual apprehension of the cosmos superior to class consciousness and expressing a deep faith in man surrounded by a "temple of eternity."[19] Unleashed poetic power sustained the reality of social illusion.

This essay was a creative debate on which path to follow, an attempt on Esenin's part to resolve the problem by relating his own ideas on poetry to folk art, and by persuading himself that the Imaginist and metaphorical character of poetry was deeply rooted in the traditional peasant method of seeing life. This synthesis, no doubt, helped him reach the conclusion that an Imaginist movement could serve both social and artistic ends simultaneously.

For their part, the Imaginists, from their beginnings in 1919 until at least 1924,[20] remained staunchly anti-Marxist, convinced that art and ideology did not mix. A perusal of statements on the topic by Anatoly Mariengof (1897–1962), Vadim Shershenevich (1893–1942), and Ivan Gruzinov (1893–1942) make this abundantly clear.[21] In the fourth and last issue of their journal *Gostinitsa dlia puteshestvuyushchikh v prekrasnom* (*The Inn for Travelers in the Beautiful*), both Mariengof and Shershenevich continued to defend creative freedom, concluding that in a society where the dominant view was rigidly materialistic, real art was either doomed to extinction or compelled to go undergound.[22] The genuine despair, often expressed in desperate language, which sounded in the poetry of the Imaginists was likewise a reflection of their concern over the increasing restraints upon free poetic expression, and their struggle against a growing dehumanization in the arts.[23]

One suspects that Esenin was attracted to the Imaginists, not only because of their outspoken support of creative freedom but also because their courageous artistic opposition to Marxism could act as a shield for his peasant dreams. Or, put simply, the movement's aesthetic orientation as expressed in its declaration of 1919 (the manifestation of life through images and metaphors of contemporary relevance),[24] appealed to him as a lyrical poet more than the emphatically ideological focus of the Scythians. Later Imaginist declarations of 1923 and 1924 similarly stressed the organic unity of metaphors, and supported the idealization and romanticization of life in an effort at a creative liberation of consciousness and feeling in the struggle for a new perception of the world.[25]

It is of interest to recall what two contemporaries have written of Esenin's links with Imaginism. Sergey Gorodetsky (1884–1967), who became an ardent exponent of communism in the twenties, wrote in 1926 that it was short-sighted for critics to berate the Imaginists' "degenerate" way of life and forget that they had played a very great role in Esenin's poetic development. The otherworldliness of Imaginism had an actual and existential (not a literary) significance for Esenin, and imparted an impetus to that idealist conception of reality expressed in "The Keys of the Soul." The Imaginist bohemian way of life did, of course, become for Esenin an alternative to a rural existence, but Imaginism had, in fact, provided his idealist vision of life and art with a literary base from which poetry could be viewed as a kind of meta-life, a metaphysical substance capable of transfiguring the fairy tale world he had known since childhood.[26]

The literary historian Ivan Rozanov had this to say of Esenin's association with the Imaginists:

He and Mariengof seemed inseparable friends. . . . It seemed to me that Esenin cherished his Imaginist friends because they were really friends, agile and enterprising, and did not suppress him with their authority, as had the "Scythians." Imaginism gave him the opportunity to cast off from his past. He was especially trying to get as far as possible away from that period when his name used to be uttered after Klyuev's. He became enraged by critics and compilers of anthologies who considered him a peasant poet. This was tantamount, he would say, to regarding the mature Pushkin as the "bard of *Ruslan and Lyudmila*." He found it *mal à propos* that poets should be grouped, not according to the devices of their art, but according to their parents and progenitors.[27]

All in all, Rozanov thought that Esenin's association with the Imaginists had been less the result of fusion (*sliianie*) than of an understanding (*soglashenie*) in the interests of effective poetic self-promotion.[28]

Rozanov, stressing the Imaginist foundation of Esenin's work as a whole, has recorded the following conversation of 1920 or 1921 between them:

The following day Esenin said to me: "I do not know why I should be paired with anyone; I am just me. It is sufficient that I belong

to the Imaginists. Many think that I am not at all an Imaginist, but
this is not true. From my very first independent beginnings I strove,
as it were by instinct or sense, toward what I have more or less
found consciously realized in the Imaginist movement. It is only
too bad that my friends have put too much faith in Imaginism,
whereas I never forget that this is only one aspect of the whole, in
fact its surface. Far more important is the poetic feeling for the
world."[29]

This last comment either anticipated or referred to one of the
early "breaks" between Esenin and his Imaginist friends (another quarrel arose in 1924 over Esenin's "high-handed" but perhaps also prankish disbandment of the Imaginist group).[30]
Esenin aired his disagreements with the Imaginists in an article
of 1921 entitled "Byt i iskusstvo" ("Social Reality and Art").
In it he attempted to distinguish himself from the group on
grounds that their poetic method was too independent of life,
too much an artificial playing with words and images without
relevance to social existence.[31]

The peremptory dismissal in 1921 of the Imaginist movement
as a superficial, inorganic literary manifestation cut off from
the life processes of the day does not stand up well after a close
reading of Imaginist poetic theory.[32] That dismissal should be
taken as no more than a momentary whim of poetic self-assertion.
It does not suggest—as some Soviet scholars have argued—that
the article "Social Reality and Art" signaled a permanent rupture
between Esenin and the Imaginists.

Any attempt to dissociate Esenin early from the Imaginists
cannot be justified. For example, the published letters Esenin
sent to Mariengof, and especially those from abroad, suggest
nothing but amicable relations between them. In fact, in the
spring of 1923 Esenin wrote him that he would publish all his
new poems only in their Imaginist journal.[33] One should also
remember that, from 1921 to 1924 and later, the Imaginists continuously defended Esenin against a Marxist criticism hostile to
the Imaginist cause. This support must be taken into account
even if one maintains that in vindicating Esenin and his poetry,
they were, at the same time, also justifying their own poetic
existence.

In words reminiscent of the writer Evgeny Zamyatin's apprehensions upon the advent of what he termed the "new catholicism"—intent on protecting the literary innocence of the Russian people as if they were still in their infancy[34]—Mariengof, in a review of "Pugachev," took contemporary Russian (read Marxist) criticism to task for its infantilism: "Unfortunately the criticism of today does not resemble a tailor but a clan of relatives: it is delighted if the fledglings in its care continue into their old age speaking with a child's voice and wearing little boys' trousers."[35] Mariengof defended the poem against hostile and immature criticism, for he viewed it as Esenin's first completely mature work. The poem he said, exhibited Esenin's genuine poetic mastery. It revealed Esenin's contemporaneity, for its lines signified the victory of Russia's peasant revolution over the rebelliousness of ancient patriarchal *Rus'*.[36]

Arseny Avraamov, a composer and literary scholar close to the Imaginists, underlined Esenin's contribution to poetic imagery: he found in his work more than fifty new images of the moon alone.[37] Another Imaginist, Ryurik Ivnev, spoke of Esenin's blood ties to Russia, and of his poetry as a way of life, a sublimation of the self.[38] Matvey Royzman characterized Esenin as the champion of the organic image in poetry.[39] Ivan Gruzinov, in order to enhance the poetic function of the Imaginists, drew a parallel between them and such eighteenth century poets as Vasily Trediakovsky, Mikhail Lomonosov, and Gavrila Derzhavin, who had to build on bare ground, and later Pushkin, the innovator. Imaginist poetic practice—or Imaginist Romanticism, as he called it—implied a poetic verbal revolution, a "blasphemous combination of words" that would free poetic thought and expression from the aesthetic and moral values of the past.[40] As for Esenin—"Esenin expresses a striving toward his native chaos, toward his fancied peasant's bast shoes, only to turn again to the forging of the forms of modern poetry, that native chaos being but artistic material for him."[41] Vadim Shershenevich, in retrospect, concluded that Esenin had never espoused any stable political ideology, but that the participation of this "Don Quixote of the Village" in the Imaginist movement had benefited both: the movement's concern with the image brought it close to his folk soul, and he in turn made Imaginist theory more precise in practice. In any case, during the period 1918–1921, when he was associated with the Imaginists, he had created his best poems.[42]

It is obvious that the Imaginists were well aware of Esenin's peasant orientation, but that they also recognized the poetic benefit to be derived from an association with him. Rozanov's formulation—that the collaboration between Esenin and the Imaginists was a mutually beneficial "understanding" rather than a fusion—may therefore be quite near the mark. This is all the more striking, if one recalls the rather vicious reaction of the Imaginists to their disbandment by Esenin and Gruzinov in 1924: at that time they denied that Esenin had ever been an ideologist of the Imaginist movement, claimed that they had always been uncertain of him as a companion-in-arms, and maintained that he had supported them only out of expediency.[43]

In the preface to the first issue of *The Inn for Travelers in the Beautiful* (1922), the Imaginists had proclaimed that the artist's task should be the seeking out and the finding of the quintessence of the beautiful, not in the elements of political programs, but in the catastrophic contemporary spiritual upheaval, in the peril of the quest for a new world view (they viewed the revolution this way, they said), and in the ingenious creation of an order of cosmic consciousness.[44]

Their Romantic search—and Esenin's as well—for the sublime in an age when revolutionary belief fell far short of poetic vision was a quixotic adventure indeed.[45]

III   *Esenin and The Symbolists*

Esenin's hostility toward the Symbolists Zinaida Gippius and Dmitry Merezhkovsky was recorded by Esenin himself in 1924–1925,[46] even though in 1915 they had received him cordially as a patriarchal and religious Russian peasant poet,[47] and Gippius had even written a favorable review of Esenin.[48]

Andrey Bely was a different matter. Although there exist only two letters from Esenin to Bely, both written in 1918 (the year of Bely's poem "Khristos voskrese" ["Christ Has Arisen"] dedicated to the revolution and included by Ivanov-Razumnik in his *Russia and Inoniya* along with two of Esenin's poems),[49] Esenin voiced his high regard for Bely as a poet and writer in his correspondence with Ivanov-Razumnik. In 1921 he spoke of

Bely's affinity for folk metaphor;[50] the next year he wrote that Bely's novel *Serebrianyi golub'* (*The Silver Dove*, 1909) was artistically far superior to anything produced by such writers as Alexey Remizov, Alexey Tolstoy, and Evgeny Zamyatin: compared to him, the latter were apprentices. In the face of Bely's lyrical digressions and his magnificent Russian, they were fit only to kiss the soles of his feet. After Nikolay Gogol, Esenin's favorite nineteenth century author, Bely was his sole joy at a time of literary decline.[51] Finally, in his "The Keys of the Soul," he described Bely's *Kotik Letaev* (1917) as art which spiritually linked the earth and the heavens.[52]

Esenin admitted his spiritual and poetic affinity to the Symbolists and their influence on him more directly in an autobiographical statement of October 1925: "Of the poets who were my contemporaries I liked most of all Blok, Bely, and Klyuev. Bely has given me much in terms of form, and Blok and Klyuev have taught me how to be lyrical."[53]

Alexander Blok recognized Esenin as a naturally gifted poet,[54] but otherwise seems not to have commented on Esenin either in his letters or diaries. He did, however, play a significant role in Esenin's life as a source of advice, encouragement, and practical assistance in starting him on his poetic career.[55]

Blok must have been attracted to Esenin by his own idealization of the "ignorant" Russian people, to whose natural, fresh, magical sense of life, to whose capacity for pagan wonder at existence, he felt strangely related as a poet. Blok felt this all the more acutely since, to his mind, these were psychic qualities that the spiritually exhausted urban Russian intelligentsia had lost.[56]

One may also surmise that Esenin, for his part, admired Blok because he shared with him a transcendental consciousness of other shores. Poetry and life were interchangeable quantities to them, and Esenin may have responded to the Symbolist and existential intent of Blok's poetry. For both, poetic expression became the pilgrimage of a spirit alienated from this world, an estrangement that turned into tragic frustration and eventual spiritual failure.

In his obituary of Valery Bryusov written in 1924, Esenin referred to him as a teacher, and remarked that with his passing,

Symbolism had finally faded into oblivion.[57] In a sense, Esenin imagined himself as stepping into that vacuum: one has the distinct feeling that in quoting two lines from Bryusov Esenin was savoring his own role as one of those Huns by whom—Bryusov had said—he cheerfully expected to be crushed in the future.[58]

Bryusov, who had once described art as an act of revelation, "doors left ajar into Eternity," a process of inspired intuition liberating man from the causal nexus of life, a poet for whom art had been a mystical key to cosmic enigmas,[59] considered Esenin an Imaginist. He said Esenin belonged to a poetic school that had rejected poetic musicality and ideological content (*ideinost'*) in favor of the image. The postrevolutionary period, which, he wrote, abounded with poetic schools capable of genuine artistic achievement, was but a preparatory stage, an inspired search given impetus by the revolution, for a new poetic language, a new perception of the world in modern poetry. Hence the Imaginists, like other contemporary literary groups, were only one of several tributaries flowing into a national stream of new artistic expression destined to create a comprehensive revolutionary art in the centuries to come.[60] (In retrospect, and in view of later Soviet creative development, Bryusov's prophecy leaves one with a sense of tragic irony.)

Two years later, in an article entitled "Vchera, segodnia i zavtra russkoi poezii" ("The Yesterday, Today, and Tomorrow of Russian Poetry"), Bryusov still described Esenin as a "prominent Imaginist" who had begun as a peasant poet. The poetry Esenin wrote between 1916 and 1921, he observed, retained a greater emotional spontaneity than did the poems of his Imaginist companions, whose influence, Bryusov felt, had been detrimental to Esenin. Esenin's lucid images, melodious lines, and light, though monotonous, rhythms distinguished him from Imaginism. Bryusov was delighted with his pure and lyrical poetry of mood, and spoke of those "excellent poems" in which Esenin had given vent to his sorrow over the ruin of his beloved village world by the city, that "iron guest."[61]

Bryusov sought artistic unity—no doubt a Symbolist penchant— at a time of artistic and cultural diversity. Seeing Esenin the Imaginist as an infinitesimal part of a future cultural mosaic, he simultaneously drew a dividing line between him and the

Symbolist age, which had enjoyed a sense of cultural unity in its artistic, mystic, and even social perception of life in the universe. Hence, Bryusov would never have agreed with Ivanov-Razumnik that Esenin was the last poet of a golden age, even thought he found the latter's nostalgia for a rural past most appealing. The title of his article leads one to suspect that he saw Esenin, not as the Hun that Esenin fancied himself to be, but as a transient poetic phenomenon suspended between yesterday and tomorrow.

IV *Esenin and Nikolay Klyuev*

The Old Believer and peasant poet Nikolay Klyuev (1887–1937) was a very important influence in Esenin's life. Sergey Gorodetsky has described Klyuev's tremendous impact not only on Esenin, but also on other writers and poets, including himself.

Esenin met Klyuev in the autumn of 1915.[62] Gorodetsky recalled that Esenin had been so taken by Klyuev's deeply felt philosophy of life, the idealist character of his poetic village imagery, that he "latched on to him" immediately. In the end Klyuev monopolized Esenin.[63] From Esenin, we learn that it was Klyuev—and not Gorodetsky, as Gorodetsky maintained—who helped him find a publisher for his first collection of poems, *Mourning for the Dead*.[64]

Others noted Klyuev's power over Esenin. One of Esenin's friends of that time, Vladimir Chernyavsky, observed that after Esenin began to move away from Gorodetsky in November of 1915, Klyuev became the major influence upon him: that influence was especially strong in 1916.[65] Ivan Rozanov spoke of Klyuev's strange and overpowering hold over Esenin in 1916.[66] We may also recall Esenin's acknowledgment, noted above, that Klyuev had taught him how to be lyrical.[67]

Undoubtedly they were attracted to each other by their peasant origin, their dreams of a spiritual rebirth of peasant Russia, their antipathy to the "educated upper classes," and a certain peasant acumen and slyness that fostered a tendency to cash in on the gullibility of city intellectuals ready to romanticize peasant Russia.[68] But whatever the reasons for their mutual attraction—Klyuev's homosexual tendency seems to have been one motivation[69]—Klyuev's hold over Esenin lasted until Esenin's death.[70]

If Klyuev did leave, as can be assumed, critical material on Esenin in his correspondence and literary remains, it has so far not become available. To establish his views on Esenin, one must resort to his poetry, which has been published in the West.[71]

The essence of Klyuev's criticism of Esenin was the latter's self-betrayal as a peasant poet. He therefore, in a negative way, affirmed Esenin's peasant roots.

In early 1922 Klyuev published his longer poem "Chetvertyi Rim" ("The Fourth Rome"), a poetic formulation of his own position as opposed to Esenin's.[72] He believed that Esenin had betrayed his peasant heritage by going over to the dandified Imaginist camp. He rejected the poetic fame Esenin sought, in top hat and lacquered shoes, at the expense of selfhood.[73] Klyuev wrote that he at least would remain true to himself, even though his soul's bark, like Esenin's, had a leak in it:

> I don't want to plug the hole in the bark of my soul
> With top hat and lacquered shoes!
> Like a meadow I blossom into horsed roof ridges of old,
> Into the smile of lakes in my song-filled silence.
> And I am faithful to my weeping, native cradle,
> To the sight of the threshing floor and my mother's grave.
> But then, to my trough where there's love and there's springtime
> Seraphim come, like goldfinches flying.
> And the bird of immortality and a swarm of ages
> Alight on my oak singing with leaves,
> And wizards have gathered at the charmed cauldrons
> To brew the immeasurable in the shell of my skull.[74]

Klyuev reflected that his own poetry would remain eternal because he remained rooted in ancient Russian tradition. His poetry was akin to a life force, one that would overcome the world of steel and factories. It was through this force that peasant Russia would merge with communism, nature triumphing over artifice, and ancient Russia over the new Russia. He characterized his poetry as pagan and national, anarchic and heretic, natural and transcendental, and almost alien to the times. But this kind of poetic power would ultimately, he believed, conquer a poetry that had betrayed its mission.[75]

Klyuev's poem "Plach o Esenine" ("Lament over Esenin")[76]—
published on December 28, 1926, a year after Esenin's suicide—
reiterated the charge of betrayal.[77] And yet the work as a whole
expressed a deep tenderness for Esenin. In metaphorical language, Klyuev claimed that he had molded and strengthened
Esenin morally, intellectually, and poetically, but that he had
fallen victim to the revolution, to the Imaginists' bohemian
way of life, and to his women.[78] Esenin, that otherworldly
cherub, was driven by the "magpie of success and terror," by
the city's accolades and also by its hostile indifference, into
Moscow's taverns.[79] He had been intimidated, Klyuev felt, by
the shameless, deceptive, and evil times (*likhie goda*).[80] But
in the end, Klyuev envisaged Esenin's spiritual return to his
native soil, after death,[81] and suggested (thinking very likely as
much of himself as of Esenin) that one could not escape one's
fate as a poet.[82]

Klyuev saw Esenin's moral dilemma as a psychological failure
to fulfill that which nature and upbringing had presumably
instilled in him. Poetic impotence followed. To Klyuev, for whom
betrayal was one of the seven spiritual "terrors" that could visit
man,[83] Esenin had betrayed the "secret culture of the Russian
people," had transgressed against their innate knowledge of a
coming earthly peasant paradise, the road to which had long
ago been symbolized by the carved wooden horses' heads atop
the front gables of Russian peasant huts.[84] By an act of faith then,
and by their poetic and spiritual kinship, Klyuev nevertheless
affirmed that, kindred spirits that they were, both he and Esenin
would still be remembered in times to come.[85]

V *Esenin and the Formalists*

The Formalists were less charitable to Esenin than was Klyuev.
Viktor Shklovsky, a member of the Formalist *Opoiaz* group
(The Society for the Study of Poetic Language), touched on
Esenin in an essay of 1924.[86]

Shklovsky disapproved of the fact that in contemporary literature *theme* (his italics) took up too much room, crowding out
technique, method, and the absorption of culture that accompanied them. Theme alone did not demand progressive self-

education and development, skill and craftsmanship. It needed
only an autobiographical, existential pumping of the self. Hence,
the greatest danger facing contemporary writers, Shklovsky
thought, was that their times did not force them to acquire
culture, and that premature technical skill therefore became
their greatest enemy.[87]

Esenin, unfortunately, belonged to the category of uncul-
tured writers. His *theme* had driven him into the tavern, and
a poetic theme could be a nail on which one could either hang a
hat or hang oneself. It was his misfortune to have worn his peasant felt boots in the city for too long. For Esenin, art was no
branch of culture, no summation of knowledge and craftsmanship
with an expanded autobiography. The theme of his poetry was
himself—lost, doomed, perishing as a poet—a theme that was as
difficult for him to bear as was wearing felt boots in summer.
He wrote no poems, but only developed his theme in the form of
poems. His inability to distinguish between skill and theme
was possibly the blunder of a peasant who had always lived
with an eye to festive occasions only.[88]

The Formalist critic Yury Tynyanov also discussed Esenin in
1924. He saw the age as one in which the powerful momentum
of prose had slowed the general progress of poetry. Hence
poetry—and with it new perceptions of reality—could only flourish during those intervals when the momentum of prose diminished. Esenin was a highly characteristic manifestation of such
an interval (*promezhutok*).[89]

Esenin's previous work had been deeply traditional, deriving
from the work of the nineteenth-century poet Afanasy Fet, from
a conventional poetic populism, and from Blok, primitively understood and filtered through Klyuev. Esenin's strength did not
lie in novelty, his leftist orientation, or his independence. Even
less convincing was his kinship with the Imaginists, who were
neither novel nor independent. His strength lay instead in the
emotional tone of his lyrical poetry. His basic poetic inspiration derived from a naive, primordial (*iskonnaia*), unusual, and
vital (*zhivuchaia*) poetic emotion. His entire poetic creativity
amounted to a continuous attempt to embellish naked emotion.
Thus his church slavonicisms, his traditional peasant Christ, and
his abusive language taken from the Imaginists promoted only

this single aim of ornamentation. An art based on primordial emotion was always closely connected with individuality, and Esenin's personality came through, in "Pugachev," for instance, allowing the reader to glimpse the man in Esenin. But his poetic personality had become so enlarged as to border on the illusive. The reader treated his poems like documents or letters received through the mail. This was, of course, good, and made for poetic power; but it was also dangerous, because poetic personality might come to live a life of its own, quite apart from the poetry, and the poetry then would turn out to be poor.

Esenin's literary personality, on the other hand, left much to be desired. Profoundly shaped by literary influences, it almost seemed borrowed, an unusually schematized Blok made worse, or a parody of Pushkin. Still, Tynyanov conceded that Esenin's emotionally charged poetic personality was powerful enough to become an original literary fact, going beyond the actual words.[90]

In his last poems—(after *Tavern Moscow*)—the hooligan did penance, however, and repented of his scandals, thereby weakening the dramatic tension of his poetry. It developed that, once the poetic personality no longer acted as a screen for his poetry, the latter was exposed in all its "literariness." The reader suddenly realized that the literariness of Esenin's poems had all along been concealed by his primitive emotionalism, and the almost tiresome, intrusive spontaneity of his poetic personality. Esenin now at times resembled an "anthology" of poets from Pushkin to the present.[91]

But did an emotive poet, Tynyanov asked, have the right to be banal in order to be momentarily effective? The answer was obviously no, if in the process of making his poetry an expression of simple, primordial emotion, Esenin's poetry had become a disappointing utilization of exhausted traditions, a collection of commonplaces that could in no way take the place of poems. Banality became so epic and so thorough as to surpass even previous banalities. Poetic intonation became a lie, and the poem, addressed to no one, expressed only a general poetic intonation, which had become inert. Poetry of this caliber pointed toward the flatness of the simplified poetry written at the end of the nineteenth century.

Tynyanov concluded that Esenin had lost his unique voice.

His attempt to test its resonance during the "interval" had failed. His poetic resonance had deceived him, and his poetry was fit for light reading only.[92]

It is natural, in view of the Formalist aesthetic premises, that its critics should have displayed a marked hostility toward Esenin. Interested in literary form per se, in the poetic transformation of reality (*ostranenie*) by means of autonomous poetic signs whose semantic, rhythmic, and euphonic identities differed from the usual "referents" of these signs or words, and negating the creative function of personality in favor of an "impersonal" though inventive manipulation of the poetic material at hand (*priem*),[93] they could not accept a Esenin, whose poetry was so much an expression of himself.

VI *Esenin and the Futurists*

The Futurist Aleksey Kruchenykh belonged to the more experimentalist wing of Russian Futurism. He had also signed many of the prerevolutionary collective Futurist manifestoes that stressed the poetic and self-sufficient nature of words and the modern poet's inalienable right to follow his own creative intuition without regard for artistic tradition.[94]

Postrevolutionary Futurism, centered in a group called LEF (Left Front of Art) that included Vladimir Mayakovsky, Osip Brik, Nikolay Aseev, and Kruchenykh, existed intermittently between 1923 and 1929. In a basic sense LEF wished to relinquish as few of its prerevolutionary theoretical links with Futurism as possible, while at the same time maintaining itself by serving the interests of a proletariat whose reactionary view of art was alien to the spirit of Futurism.[95]

As a theoretician, Kruchenykh was particularly interested in what he and Velimir Khlebnikov termed "trans-sense" language (*zaumnyi iazyk,* or *zaum'*). This was an attempt, through "whimsically fanciful and crafty combination" of cut up words, to achieve a linguistic dynamism that would overcome inert usage,[96] they explained in 1913. In a declaration of 1921, published in 1922, both men defined trans-sense poetry as an attempt to catch in a sound or image associated with the initial stage of poetic creative experience, the evanescent essence of an inspired poetic condition (somewhat like recording dream logic and content before it is obliterated by the waking consciousness). *Zaum'* became unbound poetic sense, freed from the burden of reducing a sudden poetic experience to meaningful words. To paraphrase the meaning of the experiment, one might say that *zaum'* was a process whereby poetic *Ur-sense* became translated into a contemporary *Non-sense* form.[97]

Although Kruchenykh's criticism of Esenin in 1926 can also be viewed in the light of "Eseninism" (see Chapter 11), it is sufficiently distinctive per se to be discussed in its own right.

We know very little about the relationship between Kruchenykh and Esenin. But the excessive number of critical works on Esenin published by Kruchenykh privately over a short space of time leads one to suspect that perhaps much more (e.g., poetic emulation, group interest, political ingratiation) than merely critical interest on Kruchenykh's part was involved in the relationship between these two men. Kruchenykh's Formalist and psychoanalytic method did bear critical fruit, but there is little doubt that he also employed his method to discredit Esenin morally and artistically. Whether this was for personal or political "Futurist" reasons is open to debate.

Kruchenykh's most characteristic criticism of Esenin and his poetry is contained in *Chernaia taina Esenina* (*Esenin's Dark Secret*, 1926), in which he wrote that Esenin had aways been a poet of suicide, hopelessness, and insoluble despair. Death as the only reality was his life-long theme. This proved beyond a doubt that the ominous figure of his "black man" had been assuming shape throughout his previous poetry. Esenin's melancholy at the destruction of his old village world was symptomatic of a death wish innate in Esenin's poetic nature. Contemporary criticism had either failed or did not wish to notice this. And yet only through an analysis of the dark side of his poetry could his life, his art, and his suicide be made intelligible. Kruchenykh made the very interesting observation that the hidden springs of Esenin's psyche were first revealed in his poetry before they became a real fact of existence. Consequently, Esenin lived his poetry to its predetermined and fateful end.[98]

Referring to Freud and the experience of psychiatry, Kruchenykh argued that Esenin himself had created the image that destroyed him. Hence, only a psychoanalyst or psychiatrist could come to grips with Esenin's poetic imagination, and not a literary critic. He analyzed "The Black Man," finding it to be a product of delirium and hallucination experienced by a deranged mind. It was, in effect, a poetic diary of Esenin's most intimate self; cynical, afraid of love and of women, lacking love of country. The poem's images were fed by a persecution complex, not Imaginism, and aggravated by his *delirium tremens.* As such, they were cynical in nature.[99]

Kruchenykh thus saw Esenin as a lonely man, rootless and lost in time, with neither social nor literary links. His poetry had no value for contemporary Soviet society, and its uselessness left him with psychosis and suicide as his only way out.[100]

Kruchenykh's other writings on Esenin pursued the same aim, and made similar points in various forms.[101] He was perceptive in suggesting that Esenin's poetic "heroes" in the *Tavern Moscow* poems were hostile to a revolution that had deceived them in their dreams of a return to ancient, pre-Petrine Russia. Hence, the essence of *Tavern Moscow* lay in its "exaltation of drunken debauch," and his most frightening poems were really his best.[102] His village was a Romantic contrivance to cover his rootlessness, his poetic technique was slipshod and careless as his own attitude toward life, his poetry was as indifferent to people as to human suffering, and love for him was a contagion.[103]

Kruchenykh made a final attempt to discredit Esenin in the eyes of posterity, ridiculing his effeminate, infantile perception of the world, his conception of socialism as a pagan-Christian paradise reminiscent of nineteenth century Slavophile views. He chided him for poetic imitativeness, and called him an "anthology of banalties."[104] And in a short 1927 commentary on an article by the Marxist Nikolay Bukharin, printed in the issue of *Pravda* for January 12, 1927, he quoted approvingly Bukharin's words to the effect that Esenin's drunken, sobbing poetry expressed the Russian's slavish, historical past, and disqualified him as a Soviet poet.[105]

Kruchenykh's unmistakable political nods in the direction of Marxism (Esenin's poetic prestige was rapidly sinking in official eyes) also marked earlier Futurist criticism of Esenin's work. As early as 1922 the Futurist poet Nikolay Aseev had published

an article on Esenin. Aseev's criticism of Esenin, voiced from
a standpoint sympathetic to Marxist aesthetics, confirmed Shershenevich's observation that the Futurist poet's creative perception was oriented toward an urban sensibility at variance with
a pastoral perception of the world.[106]

Aseev recognized Esenin's poetic gift, but criticized his unhealthy tendency to return to patriarchal Russia. His poetry, he
said, moved on a wave of lyricism only, at the expense of contemporary (Marxist) social awareness. Aseev found fault with
Esenin's wistfulness and the "idiotically sly grin of the holy
fool" in his poem "Pugachev"; he also attacked a collection
of his religious poetry published by the Scythians in 1920 in
Berlin.[107]

Aseev believed that Esenin had reached a crossroads in "The
Keys of the Soul": thereafter he could either fall into the depths
of the formal method—by which Aseev presumably meant an
art devoid of social content, a "superficially mystical" poetry—or
he could, with the help of Marxist criticism, arrive at contemporary social awareness. Aseev viewed with disfavor Esenin's rejection of Marxist class consciousness and guardianship in art, and
frowned upon his permitting folklore devices to act as the sole
organizing principle of poetic work. In elevating the poet's
consciousness of an eternal principle motivating art above class
consciousness, Esenin became a "mystagogue" as it were, a high
priest guarding the keys to an inner sanctum. This, Aseev believed, led inescapably to Symbolism, with its inherent tendency
toward paganism and artistic mysticism. Esenin's interest in the
art of ancient Russian ornamentation (Aseev said nothing of
Esenin's straining at poetic truisms) could only diminish his
capacity for absorbing the revolutionary present.[108]

Much later, when Aseev published a study of "The Black
Man" (he had heard Esenin read it two weeks before his suicide), his critical apprehensions apparently had been proved
correct. The poem, Aseev said, exhibited Esenin in all his human
vulnerability, without his artificial nationalism. There he yearned
for human warmth and yet could not suppress his cold despair,
the pain and the terror that lay in wait for him in the empty
fields signifying his spiritual isolation. Aseev, however, could not
deny that in the final analysis Esenin was a poet of his epoch.

The past, not the future, had disoriented his creative power and he paid with his life for his attempt to convey the new in his poetry.[109]

Esenin never quite got along with Vladimir Mayakovsky (1893–1930), as was the case with anyone in whom he sensed great poetic talent. And yet there did exist, despite all their differences, a spiritual and poetic bond between them: the common experience of carrying the seed of self-destruction within them, an experience that left profound traces on their poetic work. It is probable that Mayakovsky's criticism of Esenin and his suicide was motivated by an inner recognition of a kindred spirit's fate, by an awareness of the hazards of poetic creation in the shadow of death, by a knowledge that perhaps only initiates share.

An analysis of Mayakovsky's longer prerevolutionary poems shows that the rate of incidence of the suicide motif in them was continuously on the increase.[110] Had the revolution of 1917 not provided Mayakovsky (as it did Esenin) with an outlet for his spiritual anarchism and iconoclasm (traits also characteristice of Esenin's poetry of 1917–1918), he might very well have committed suicide earlier. Instead, he delayed the fatal hour because he came to believe for a time that this poetic impulse could be put at the service of the State, just as Esenin wrongly believed that his poetry too could serve the revolution. But when poetic nature proved Mayakovsky wrong, he finally did what his poetry had been prophesying for a lifetime. There is indeed much that binds the tragedies of these two Russian poets together.

The account in Mayakovsky's essay, "Kak delat' stikhi" ("How to Make Poetry") of how he wrote the poem "Sergeiu Eseninu" ("To Esenin," 1926), his quite *desperate* need to counter the effect of the last two lines of Esenin's suicide poem, is not only an extraordinary event in the history of the creative process, but also strongly suggests that Mayakovsky was here speaking not so much for the state as for himself; that in his poetic rebuttal of Esenin's poem, he was fighting for his very existence; that the outcome of the battle for him was a matter of life or death.

Esenin had written in the two lines in question: "There is

nothing novel about dying in this world. / For that matter, living isn't novel any more either."[111]

In his essay, Mayakovsky wrote that when Esenin's suicide became a literary fact, he realized it would bring many other such vacillating spirits to suicide. Esenin's last two lines in particular could only be neutralized by poetry. He wanted to substitute for the "easy prettiness of death" that they implied another kind of beauty, a paean to the joy of life necessary to a proletarian humanity in the realization of its revolutionary aims. His poem took shape only slowly. The antidotal two lines emerged only after he had composed some fifty to sixty variants.[112]

In the poem itself, written in March of 1926, Mayakovsky spoke with obvious sympathy and tenderness. Sorrow stuck in his throat like a lump, he confessed. He could not agree with those critics who blamed Esenin's suicide upon his classless bohemianism. With much irony, Mayakovsky remarked that a proletarian-minded, class-conscious Esenin, fulfilling his daily poetic norm, would have committed suicide even sooner. But he did berate Esenin for increasing the number of suicides, and lamented the fact that, in Esenin, the Russian people, themselves creators of language, had lost a sonorous though good-for-nothing apprentice. Unlike Esenin, he felt that there was much too much to do in life, and that life had first to be transformed before it could be exalted. It had to be made, it could not just be taken.

Mayakovsky implied that Esenin had taken the easy way out. He agreed that the times were difficult for the pen, but asked whether the path of a great (*sic*) man had ever been easy. The poetic word was the pilot star of human potential energy: its function was to destroy the past, which interfered with the realization of revolutionary ideals. Our planet was little made for joy, and joy had to be torn from the clutches of future days.[113] Then came Mayakovsky's last two lines, which—in view of his own suicide some four years later—seem less an antidote to Esenin's lines than an affirmation of a truth for which both poets in the end laid down their lives:

> In this life
> > it is not difficult to die.
> To build a life however
> > is considerably harder.[114]

VII   *Esenin and the Academic Critics:*
       Kravtsov and Neyman

Many literary critics with an academic background looked
at Esenin's work in the light of folk tradition.[115] Two of these,
Nikolay Kravtsov and Boris Neyman, devoted some effort to
an analysis of the folklore roots of his poetic imagery.

Nikolay Kravtsov (1906–   ), a folklore specialist who has
been a professor at Moscow State University since 1962 and
who has worked mainly on Slavic literatures and folklore,[116]
in 1926 published a very interesting analysis of the connection
between Esenin's poetic work and folklore.[117]

Kravtsov pointed out that Esenin used the folklore method
of psychological parallelism as a poetic device, but that his
depiction of nature was also influenced by the nineteenth century
peasant poetry tradition and by the Symbolists.[118] He then
singled out specific folklore elements in Esenin's poetry. He
found negative parallelism: "It is not the cuckoos that have
begun to grieve– / It is Tanya's relatives that are crying";[119]
positive parallelism: "The grey pussy willows at the wattle fence /
Shall more tenderly bow their heads";[120] and psychological parallelism in popular song (*chastushka*) form: "O, little fish of
mine, little small bones! / You are peasant kids, striplings!"[121]
Kravtsov described Esenin's metaphorical creations of poetic
myth: here the poet developed anthropomorphized nature into
a legend or myth designed to explain some natural phenomenon
(as for instance in his poem "Those are not clouds roaming on
the other side of the barn," where a small round loaf of bread
baked by the Mother of God, and dropped by the infant Jesus,
becomes the moon).[122]

Kravtsov also discussed Esenin's utilization of the Russian riddle for poetic ends.[123] An important aspect of this use of riddles,
themselves based on enigmatic metaphor or simile, wrote
Kravtsov, was Esenin's reworking of them. In the process, the
solution to any one riddle provided him with new images whose
metaphoric function he further developed and transformed into
new "metaphorized simile" units. Kravtsov gave as an instance
of this a riddle that Esenin had taken from folklore collector
Dmitry Sadovnikov, where a river is the answer to: "The sleigh

is moving / But the shaft lies unused." In Esenin this produced the following lines: "The ruddy new moon, becoming a foal,/ Harnessed itself to our sleigh."[124]

In his very convincing exposition, Kravtsov dwelt at some length on Esenin's similar use of folk images that he poetically transformed. Kravtsov distinguished between the logical, conscious development of a basic image and the intermingling of developed images. In the first case, a line such as "The ruddy new moon becoming a foal" could be further consciously developed into "With the new moon's face chewing hay."[125] In the second case, the new moon as a foal capable of chewing hay, and the moon's horn from the lines "The horn of the moon drop by drop pours / Oil onto the grey undulating cabbage beds" could be united in the following lines: "The horselike moon's skull / Drips gold of decayed mica."[126]

Kravtsov found parallels between the medieval *Slovo o polku Igoreve* (*Lay of Igor's Campaign*) and some of Esenin's poems. He identified what he termed "accidental folk usages" in Esenin's poetry brought about by a theme's demands (e.g., stylistic peculiarities of folk poetry, use of folk beliefs, mythical motifs, folk song structure, and various shades of the peasant lexicon). He added that Esenin's early poetry had been written under the influence of the oral tradition of folk poetry, and that his familiarity with it could hardly have been of a bookish nature.[127]

Kravtsov concluded that the folk images in Esenin's poetry acquired other meanings and functions than those they expressed in folklore, for Esenin reworked folk material in his own way. His poetic rhythms differed from those of the Russian folk song or riddle. As an Imaginist, he naturally emphasized the role of the poetic image and—since he had begun as a peasant poet under the influence of folk poetry—it was only natural that he should use it and the riddle as sources of imagery. Psychological parallelism helped him solve the problem of the poetic function of nature; his interest in the epic aspect of folk poetry led him to develop epic themes in his poetry using folk language as a stylistic basis.[128]

The literary scholar Boris Neyman (1888–   ) also published a study of the sources of Esenin's imagery.[129] His analysis brought Neyman (who focused on Esenin's postrevolutionary poetry)

to the conclusion that Esenin had taken his poetic material, not
from immediate life experience, but from books (mainly folklore material). One could not, therefore, speak of his imagery
as emerging from a spontaneous peasant perception of the world.
In fact, Esenin had himself indicated most of his sources in
"The Keys of the Soul" (1918):[130] he seems to have drawn
mainly on Dmitry Sadovnikov's *Riddles of the Russian People*
and Alexander Afanasev's *The Slavs' Poetic Conceptions of
Nature*, but was likewise familiar with the work of other folklore scholars such as Vladimir Stasov, Fedor Buslaev, and Alexander Potebnya.[131]

Neyman gave detailed examples from Esenin's poetry of
straightforward borrowing from riddles with scarcely any
changes. Next he identified images that, though not actually
found in any one riddle, were motivated by suggestive images
found in riddles: thus the image of stars resembling fish found in
"Inoniia" (II, 42) could have been suggested by a riddle in
which the sun's rays are compared to a golden pike. Neyman
saw these images as perhaps unconscious transpositions of the
function of image from one object or manifestation of nature
to another.[132] He gave examples of such metaphorical development of folklore material through associative thinking: the moon-
steed (*Kon'-mesiats*) of folklore poetry might have been transformed into a sun-steed to produce the image of the sun freezing
like a puddle of urine left behind by a gelding.[133].

Neyman then considered Esenin's poetic material, whose
source, he believed, was other than the riddle. He indicated the
mythological origins of his poetry, showing what use he made
of such basic images as the sun, the new moon, the cloud, and
the rainbow.[134] For example, Esenin's use of the sun as a
plough in "Inoniia" (II, 38) might very well have come from
Buslaev, who mentions such an image.[135]

These traits of Esenin's poetics were by no means accidental
or insignificant. Of course, in many instances Esenin developed
borrowed images independently. But folk poetic inspiration remained a constant in his work, although with an occasional
rhythmic reworking of the sources. Taking Esenin's poem "Song
about Bread" (1921) as an indicative example, Neyman argued
for the view (shared, he said, by another folklore specialist,

Pavel Sakulin) that the riddle was a far more productive source of Esenin's imagery than the *Lay of Igor's Campaign*. It was also characteristic of Esenin that the enigmatic quality of a borrowed image did, in the process of poetic creation, assume the simpler, more everyday contours of rural existence. Neyman saw Esenin's poetry as a synthesis of ineffable mystery and that wonderful peasant warmth peculiar to him.[136]

Both Kravtsov and Neyman investigated the nature of Esenin's creative process and the degree of his poetic originality (only Kravtsov credited Esenin with poetic originality), and concluded that the folklore sources of poetic material had essentially motivated his writing.

CHAPTER 10

Marxists

I Esenin and Voronsky

IN his "Autobiography" of June 20, 1924, Esenin explained
that he had welcomed the first phase of the revolution sym-
pathetically, but more "elementally than consciously."[1] Marxist
literary criticism of Esenin and his poetry after 1917 was a
lengthy attempt to retain what could be salvaged of Esenin
for the revolution.

One of the most outstanding Marxist critics of the 1920s,
and one of the chief architects of the literary coalition with
the Fellow Travelers,[2] was Alexander Voronsky (1884–1943).
The son of a priest and a student at a religious seminary, he
joined the Social Democratic Party at the age of nineteen and
entered party underground work, for which he was several
times imprisoned and exiled. In 1921 he founded the journal
Krasnaia nov' (*Red Virgin Soil*), which he edited until 1927.
He also edited the journal *Prozhektor* (*The Projector*) from
1922 on, and worked in the State Publishing House. He began
to realize, however, that the revolutionary ideals he had fought
for were being betrayed, especially after Lenin's death in 1924
and the rise of Stalin. Hence he sympathized with Trotsky's
opposition party from 1925 to 1928; as a man of honesty and
integrity, he was expelled from the Communist Party in 1927.
In the early 1930s he was arrested several times and exiled.
Allowed to return to Moscow and work in the State Publishing
House's classical literature section, in ill health, he discontinued
his critical activity altogether to devote himself to his memoirs
and a book on Gogol, his life-long interest. The book was
confiscated for deviationism, and he himself imprisoned and
repressed in 1937. He was rehabilitated posthumously after
the Twentieth Party Congress in 1956.[3]

As a critic Voronsky tried to combine his own intuitive view of a classless, objective, imagist creative process—very reminiscent of Bely and Symbolist aesthetics[4]—with Marxist prescriptiveness. His approach drew heavily upon his conviction that proletarian culture and art could not be created in a vacuum that rejected the cultural achievements of the past and the literary services of the Fellow Travelers in the present. If there was no proletarian culture, there was a proletarian consciousness and orientation, whose temporary function in a transitional epoch of "the dictatorship of the proletariat" was to create a ruthless revolutionary fighter by reeducating the workers, peasants, and intelligentsia; a fighter, moreover, whose revolutionary love was as great as was his hatred of everything that hindered the achievement of a future classless society. Hence the main proletarian driving force of that time had nothing in common with the socialist art of the future, which would be motivated by more integrated, peaceful, and humanitarian purposes and which would have absorbed the best of both the art of past ages and that of the proletarian phase. He criticized proletarian groups for making the lives of the Fellow Travelers difficult in order to establish their own monopoly in art and literature. He considered the Fellow Travelers as yet ideologically weak, but thought that they were by far the most talented group of writers existing in Soviet Russia, and that they could be of valuable service to the revolution because their artistic methods and work grew out of the cultural wealth of the past. He emphasized the need for artistic method because, after all, art could not be viewed simply, he argued, as the expression of an ideology with propaganda value. He invited the party, therefore, to mitigate the hostility toward Fellow Travelers by taking control of proletarian groups. It was unfair, he wrote, to expect ideological purity from nonparty writers, though the ideological deviations of many of them had to be countered firmly and decisively. He urged the amalgamation of diverse Communist groups, which would remain creatively independent but simultaneously be under the political and cultural aegis of the party. He hoped that, in time, other groups such as the Fellow Travelers might join in. Such a move would clear the literary atmosphere; political censorship (which he considered of prime importance) would eliminate undesirable counterrevolutionary trends and yet permit a sufficient degree of elasticity and freedom for the development of a revolution-oriented art.[5]

Robert Maguire, who has published a study of Voronsky and his journal, detects a shift in Voronsky's theory of literature between 1924 and 1927. The shift was toward a Romantic, idealist aesthetics and entailed reevaluation of the nature of the creative process as primarily aesthetic rather than predominantly sociological. The creative process as such became for Voronsky an intuitive, spontaneous, objective, and impersonal one (a view which basically had already been expressed in his 1923 article on the process of artistic cognition), independent both of the artist's volition and of sociological criteria. This creative experience could be revealed only to those endowed with a special poetic perception which saw a cosmos more real and beautiful than that which could be derived from a cognitive, empirical artistic approach to the world.[6]

In an article on the artist in Soviet society dated November 1921, first published in 1922[7] and republished in his 1923 collection of articles *Na styke* (*At the Meeting Point*), Voronsky hit out against religious, mystical moods in poetry and literature because, anemic and deadening, they would emasculate art. He was concerned that the religious element—in which he discerned sickness and disease—would obstruct the growth of the young and healthy shoots of the revolution. He also feared that decadence, that philistine, bourgeois way of life, would, for lack of bolshevik resistance, erase the very memory of revolutionary ideas once fought for.[8] He was aware, he wrote, that years of revolution involving armies, collectives, and classes were not very conducive to the poetic word, which was linked with the individual, the personal, and the intimate (*svoe*). Still, any literature or poetry should be alive and sincere (*iznutra*); it should be about the little man, but it should also deal with the great revolutionary principles that were at stake.[9]

Voronsky pointed to the extremely meager output of contemporary literature, admitted that contemporary creative sensibilities had been shaken by the revolutionary upheaval, and argued for maintaining cultural continuity with the past. The new literary forces could only benefit from contact with the older generation of writers in the Soviet Union who still followed their calling. But art, he emphasized, could not be apolitical: the apolitical artist was creatively dead no matter how gifted he was. Art needed an aim, although it must not become tendentious. With many talented Russian writers now living in the West, and in order to combat religious mysticism, philistinism, and pure Formalism in art, the young generation of Soviet writers needed above all a minimum of moral and sociopolitical acumen (*imet' iziuminku, "boga zhivogo cheloveka"*), for otherwise they would certainly find themselves in the camp of the enemies of labor.[10]

But Voronsky was optimistic enough to believe that eventually new writers and readers would emerge, even though at present the times made their appearance difficult:

The new reader and the new writer will come. We are now experiencing an especially painful phase of exhaustion, impoverishment, collapse, and this has affected the spiritual condition of both the new readers and the new writers who are in the process of being born. When the cannons speak, the voice of the skald cannot be heard. Sagas are composed after battle. And when a deadening hunger oppresses the land, it is difficult to be inspired.[11]

The new readers and writers, the new intelligentsia, would undoubtedly spring from the people, and this, he mused, might constitute the beginning of a revolutionary Romanticism. In any case, the revolution could not afford to ignore those writers who might still align themselves with the revolutionary cause and enrich it with their individual talents. But he was afraid, he confessed, that the necessary transmission of past cultural values to future generations by the new revolutionary class was in danger of being delayed by the raging conflict between the old and the new.[12]

In the November 1921 article, Esenin had caught Voronsky's eye, no doubt, as one of these new poets. Referring in particular to Esenin's poem "Wolf's End," the critic noted a certain militant despair in Esenin's thematic juxtaposition of a doomed

village world dear to him and the hostile city.[13] Writing later
in 1924, Voronsky realized that it was precisely this conflict
between past and present that characterized Esenin's poetry.
In the final analysis, Voronsky wrote, the past as poetic theme,
his preoccupation with the old Russian peasant way of life,
had energized Esenin's poetry.[14]

In this article of 1924, Voronsky discussed chiefly Esenin's
poetic development in relation to the revolution. Esenin, he
said, was incapable of writing socially conscious poetry. His
descriptions of village life were idyllic, and did not reflect the
actual village with its excessive toil and turmoil, its hard life
and social hatreds. The revolution was foreign to him, and he
himself was a poet alienated from his times. Voronsky criticized
Esenin for failing to understand the social and cultural function
of revolutionary socialism: the proletarian revolution would
encourage socialist industrialization, which in turn would free
millions of people from labor and enable them to apply themselves to higher and more rewarding levels of human activity.
Esenin did not realize that the revolution would free man
both from his subordination to the machine and from the
dependence on chance that was so central a factor in an
unindustrialized, agricultural society. He did not understand
that the revolution wanted to make man the envied center of
creation. Being apolitical, he did not foresee that the real
salvation of the village—even though its burden was unbearably
heavy to bear in a transitional epoch—lay in joining forces
with the revolutionary working class.[15]

As a direct consequence of his social blindness and political
naïveté, Esenin's "Inoniia" could not combine his dreams of a
peasant paradise on earth with the aims of the proletarian
revolution. "Inoniia" was therefore a superficial, unreal phan-
tasmagoria whose utopian vision lacked concreteness and poetic
unity. It was not a product of genuine poetic inspiration, but
merely a toying with words and images. This made for one
negative aspect of the poem's Imaginism. Foreign to the essentially dynamic spirit of socialism, the poem exuded the spirit
of the static, stagnant, decrepit, and slumbering Orient. The
poem "Prayer for the Dead," written in an antitechnological
vein, was similarly conservative in spirit, regressive and anti-

socialist. In "Pugachev" and "Land of Scoundrels" the past battled with the present: the peasant defended his old way of life, trying to ward off the new Soviet age of progress, but, like Pugachev, perished in the process. Esenin's *Tavern Moscow* poems were decadent because they expressed a loss of faith in the creative potential of the revolution. They reflected spiritual prostration, a profound antisocial disposition, and the breakdown of personality. Since this was so, the revolution had to combat them, because their mood could damage both communist youth and revolutionary literature.[16]

Voronsky discerned a duality of spirit, a split personality in Esenin, a dichotomy between his peasant roots and the Soviet revolutionary era that he seemed *unwilling to resolve*; instead, he *consciously* exploited this duality (Voronsky's emphasis). Esenin's reluctance to overcome his inner discord made his poetry all the more harmful to the reader. Hooliganism thrived side by side with humility and kindheartedness, a yearning for the countryside was countered by a yen for the city, religiousness alternated with blasphemy, a sensitive, enrapturing lyricism coexisted with a consciously rude imagery, and animality with mysticism. For Esenin this expressed the complexity of the human soul, but Voronsky explained such duality on the basis of the general class position of the peasantry, with its tendency toward either "bourgeois" reaction or "proletarian" revolution.[17]

Voronsky noted a poetic shift from Esenin's *Tavern Moscow* mood toward what was perhaps an emerging search for contemporary Soviet Russia in such poems of 1924 as "Letter to Mother," "Soviet *Rus'*," and poems from his *Persian Motifs*. The contagious sincerity and simplicity of these poems, he wrote, their profound and delicate lyricism, their emotional intensity and enthusiasm, their general tone of affirmation instead of his usual poetic flabbiness, did perhaps augur well for Esenin's future poetic development. Of course they lacked revolutionary vehemence and fervor, but Voronsky felt that, after the battle-cries of the revolution, the time had now come when such poems as these, with their deep poetic scrutiny of the surrounding world, could be appreciated by the reader. That Esenin's pure mood poetry had already attracted an enthusiastic following suggested that the epoch was both in need of, and prepared for, such poetry.

It was, however, difficult to say how serious this shift of poetic consciousness was and how long it would last. A poem such as "Stanzas," for instance, which was weak and unconvincing poetry, suggested that his shift of poetic focus contained much that was superficial and insufficiently organic. Perhaps in the end all that the revolution would obtain from Esenin would be a certain amount of utilizable hooliganism, with its characteristically peasant recklessness, boldness, and savage waste of strength, as in "Pugachev," which was close to the revolutionary epoch in spirit. But to give full vent to his extraordinary talent, Esenin would have to overcome his own Imaginist, urbanized Pugachev-dandy, whose hooliganism had little in common with the historical Pugachev. Perhaps Pushkin's influence, detectible in his latest poetry, would assist him, or the ability he displayed at making his images palpable, which indicated that he was at bottom a Realist. In retrospect, "Inoniia" was a step away from his earlier religious poetry; the poem's concrete depiction of a peasant paradise on earth represented a definite step in the direction of the real world.[18]

Voronsky was alarmed lest one of the most sensitive contemporary lyrical poets find himself doomed to a disintegration of creative personality.[19] He ended his article with an expectant but stern "fatherly" admonition:

It is probably too early yet for Esenin to write poetry about Marx and Lenin, but it would indeed be very timely and to the point for him to look into them attentively, not in jest, but in order to rework some aspects of his creative writing. It will be bad if the new stream in the poet's creative work should turn out to be only a voluntary or an involuntary accident, a tribute to the times and the product of a rake's temporary and flighty enthusiasm. Our epoch does not like jests, and does not forgive being jested with. Nor is it a secret to anyone that quite a few parasites have been spawned in our many branches of social life. This is not meant either as a reproach or as an insult to Esenin, but as a friendly and sincere warning, with one purpose in mind only, namely that he give us a good choice of poems that are consonant with our present epoch. Much will be exacted from him, to whom much has been given.

Esenin has been given much.[20]

In 1925 Voronsky had still not abandoned hope of Esenin's "political" regeneration. He did concede, however, that the rise of the new Soviet village had transformed Esenin into an alienated figure:

In one essential way Esenin has remained true to himself, to his initial motifs: he still grieves over his past youth, over withering, over the fact that life progresses and develops in its own way, paying no heed to the poet. There has been added only a more concrete feeling that the revolutionary struggle has created a new Soviet *Rus'* in place of the old *Rus'* so that even the native, quiet and stagnant village has changed, losing its former aspect. The poet sees the truth of this life, its growth and its flourishing, he retreats before it with a bow and with a gesture of welcome, retaining his "lyre" so as to sing praises to his old *"Rus'."*[21]

Almost immediately after Esenin's suicide, Voronsky published an article in which he tried to define the causes of his death. A unique, genuine artist of great power and talent, able to stir the hearts of all his readers, Esenin was not a contemporary peasant poet. He was a national poet (*natsionalen*), who wrote about the very essence of old rural Russia; but he was defeated by forces more powerful than he, chief among which was alienation. His extreme poetic self-centeredness had fed on poetry as an end in itself. He had written on inspiration alone, without cultivating poetic self-discipline and without creative roots in the social culture of his day. As a result, poetry became everything in his life, an evil sorceress who swallowed him up as a man, a warning to those who would only exploit nature's poetic gifts.[22] In a subsequent article, he reminisced in a mellower vein, recalling a conversation he had had with Esenin in the autumn of 1923. Esenin had observed then that, although he supported Soviet power and would collaborate with Voronsky, he loved his old Russia in his own way and would not permit the Communists to muzzle him creatively.[23]

But in words that no doubt sprang from his own disenchantment at the time over unrealized goals in art and literature (too little Communist sincerity, too much barren ideological art[24]), Voronsky added that there was a need for such poetry as Esenin's at a time when contemporary civilization was marked by an alarming lack of spontaneous human relationships, and stamped instead by a love for things and phantasms, by a materialist (*veshchnyi*) and ideological fetishism.[25]

II   *Esenin and Trotsky*

Lev Trotsky's stance as a literary critic—typically Marxian in its paradoxical thinking—can be gauged from the following passage of 1924. On the one hand, Trotsky defended political literary censorship: "Our standard is clearly political, . . . imperative and intolerant. But for this very reason it must define the limits of its activity clearly. For a more precise expression of my meaning, I will say: we ought to have a watchful revolutionary censorship, and a broad flexible policy in the field of art, free from petty partisan maliciousness."[26] On the other hand, he maintained that: "Art must make its own way and by its own means. The Marxian methods are not the same as the artistic. . . . The domain of art is not one in which the Party is called upon to command. It can and must protect and help art, but it can only lead it indirectly."[27] The Fellow Travelers as an intelligentsia, in Trotsky's view, were politically passive and contemplative by nature. But artistically they had portrayed the revolution better than the proletarian writers, who were too directly involved in it and who therefore lacked the necessary perspective. To be sure, the Fellow Travelers were politically unreliable. But if one eliminated such writers as Boris Pilnyak, Vsevolod, Ivanov and other "Serapion Brothers," Mayakovsky, and Esenin, there would remain only "a few unpaid promissory notes of a future proletarian literature."[28] Consequently, the party should regard existing literary Fellow Traveler groups in terms of their potential for helping to build a socialist art and culture, not as competitors of working class writers.[29]

Trotsky viewed Esenin as a peasant poet who had accepted the revolution in his own way; and the revolution had made his career by providing him with spiritual and creative poetic material. However, the Communist ideal of the revolution remained foreign to him. Instead of accepting it as a "social purposeful process," he had merely made poetic use of it as an elemental experience. Esenin's dual point of view made him socially and artistically dangerous, even though as a Fellow Traveler he was important in a literary sense.

Esenin, Trotsky wrote, looked more favorably upon the peasant than the worker, and thus expressed a new kind of Soviet populism that lacked all political perspective. Like the majority of the Fellow Traveler intelligentsia, he came from the peasantry; his intent to align the revolution with it rather than with the proletariat could only lead to a violent, bloody social and economic regression. His intent made him not a revolutionary, but a "fool of the revolution." Like all rustic writers, he inclined toward "a primitive nationalism smelling of the roach."[30]

Trotsky saw Esenin at the time as an Imaginist, but this was only a sign, he said, of his creative immaturity. Trotsky suggested that Esenin's essentially peasant aesthetics—"poetry of the repetitive forms of life" that at bottom had "little mobility" and sought "a way out in condensed imagery"—was akin to Imaginist doctrine, which lacked dynamism because of its emphasis on the self-sufficiency of the poetic image. Esenin's attempt to write an Imaginist poem in "Pugachev" failed, Trostky believed, and this demonstrated that the Imaginist path was not his. The poem's imagery was excessively heavy; as a drama it was far too lyrical, too narrative, and too descriptive. Pugachev—who was Esenin himself from "top to toe"—was a bit of a ridiculous Imaginist, one who longed to be terrible but instead was only a sentimental Romantic. In comparing Esenin to Klyuev, Trotsky noted that Esenin's peasant roots were less deep than Klyuev's, and that his poetry ultimately reflected the prerevolutionary and revolutionary spirit of peasant youth generally driven to turbulence by disrupted village life.

In Trotsky's eyes, Esenin was still a man of the future. Being a younger poet (younger than Klyuev, for instance), he was also more flexible and more open to fresh possibilities. Under the impact of the city he had become more nervous and dynamic, more responsive to the new. Esenin had begun his "wander-years," he felt, and would not thereafter be the same as before. Trotsky preferred to wait and see what the change would be.[31]

But Trotsky was also convinced that a creative intelligentsia stemming from the peasantry had a more primitive, limited, and egotistic point of view in economics, politics, and art than did the proletariat. A point of view that set Russia's age-old, organic, "national" village against the dynamic city was historically re-actionary. A peasant aesthetic and art based on such an approach was "inimical to the proletariat, incompatible with progress and doomed to extinction." As Trotsky phrased it, "such an art, even as far as form is concerned, can give nothing but rehashes and reminiscences."[32]

In January of 1926 Trotsky published a memorable article dedicated to Esenin's memory.[33] The revolutionary epoch, he wrote, had not been congenial to Esenin's tender lyrical tempera-ment, a fact that explained his suicide. Esenin had been a defenseless soul trying to cover his tenderness with a rude front. Trotsky continued:

Our epoch is a grim epoch, it is perhaps one of the grimmest in the history of so-called civilized humanity. The revolutionary born for these decades is possessed by the furious patriotism of his epoch, which is his fatherland in time. Esenin was not a revolutionary. The author of "Pugachev" and of "The Ballad about the Twenty-six" was the most intimate of lyrical poets. Our epoch, however, is not a lyrical one. In this lies the *main* reason why Sergey Esenin left us and his epoch wilfully and so early. (Trotsky's italics)[34]

Esenin's peasant background had engendered his individual weakness. Torn from the old, he had found no roots in the new, and the city had demoralized him still further. Deeply a people's (*narodnyi*) poet, he had always striven toward the revolution, only to find that it was foreign to his nature. Where he was intimate, tender, and lyrical, the revolution was public, epic, and catastrophic. As a lyrical poet, he was helpless in the face of revolutionary times, and his creative nature had been broken by the epoch. The mainsprings of the revolutionary period were mightier than individual drives. But Esenin—having reflected the times in his own way in genuine and beautiful images—belonged to the revolution as one of its future sons, to the time when the future socialist society would once again become fertile ground for the lyrical spirit.[35]

III *The Octobrists: Esenin and Lelevich*

The critic G. Lelevich (1901–1945) advocated literary hegemony for the Octobrist group of proletarian writers.[36] He believed that such literary predominance could be achieved if the party supported all those writers and poets willing to serve its political goals, and eliminated all others.[37] Or, as he put it elsewhere in 1923: *"But only the artist holding the point of view of the working class can understand the contemporary social relations.* For there cannot be any nonclass understanding of social relations."[38]

For Lelevich, Esenin's early books of poetry expressed a *kulak's* (wealthy peasant exploiter's) religious view of the world. But in such recent poems of 1924 as "Soviet *Rus'*," "The Song of the Great Campaign," and "Na rodine" ("Back Home"), his work seemed to have entered upon a transitional period. He still lacked contemporary proletarian consciousness, but he had at least become aware of the new revolutionary developments in the countryside and welcomed them joyfully (or so Lelevich thought). He sensed the alienation and uselessness of his previous poetry with respect to contemporary Soviet village life, yet could not yet free himself from the grip of the old. His new awareness was, however, a first step away from his former lack of social consciousness. He had a future only if he turned a new, revolutionary leaf in his poetic work.[39]

Lelevich amplified his view in a book on Esenin, published in 1926, in which he said that Esenin's early work reflected his ties with the peasant intelligentsia. His pantheistic poetry was attuned to both the ideology of the patriarchal, wealthy peasant class and the mystical nationalism of "aristocratic-bourgeois" (*dvoriansko-burzhuaznyi*) poetry, by which Lelevich probably meant Russian Symbolist or possibly even Acmeist poetry. Lelevich was quick to add, however, that Esenin's religious sense for the world of nature was intimately linked to his sense of native soil (*rodina*).

Lelevich noted the rebellious, elemental striving of the Russian peasantry in such poems as "Marfa the Mayoress" of 1914, remarked upon Esenin's enthusiastic but religiously tinged peasant view of the revolution as harbinger of a peasant paradise on earth, and discussed his essentially peasant hostility toward the technological culture of the city and proletarian ideology in art. That hostility, Lelevich wrote, found clear expression in "The Keys of the Soul," whose theoretical ideas on the nature of art corresponded to Esenin's poetic development.[40]

Lelevich explained Esenin's tragedy simply in terms of his failure to become a revolutionary poet. He criticized his association with the reactionary, declassed, and petty bourgeois Imaginists. He considered his "Pugachev" the best product of his Imaginist phase, but thought it overburdened with images. Lelevich reiterated his belief that only in Esenin's "Soviet *Rus'*" period had there appeared any signs of a hopeful transition. Though his revolutionary poetic attempts had been artistically weak, they were also sincere, and reflected a movement toward Pushkin's simplicity and clarity, as well as toward folk poetry. Hence "The Song of the Great Campaign"—in Lelevich's view a more significant poem of his last period—had a sustained popular song (*chastushka*) rhythm running through it, and harked back, as did other poems of this period, to Pushkin's poetic perception.[41]

IV *Esenin, Lvov-Rogachevsky, and Yakubovsky*

Esenin had caught the attention of another prominent Marxist critic earlier, in 1919. V. Lvov-Rogachevsky (1874–1930), with whom Esenin seems to have been on good terms in 1918–1919,[42] was particularly interested at the time in the relation between Russian peasant poets and proletarian poets. He saw the peasant poets as Romantics, fabulists disillusioned with present reality and consequently captivated by the otherworldly. But their creative development, he wrote, hinged on their being able to shake off the past.[43] Then again, the future, bringing with it a new proletarian culture, would be the work of decades, even centuries. The self-sufficient, militant, and myopic proletarian poets' doctrine of an instant proletarian culture, or the peasant poets' sleepy reverie and lazy inertia, could only delay this process.[44]

Lvov-Rogachevsky regarded Esenin as a peasant Symbolist who used transcendental images. Esenin, he thought, was closely linked to Fedor Tyutchev, Konstantin Balmont, Bely, and Blok, and he cited Esenin's poem of 1917 "Pesnia, lug, reki zatony" ("Song, meadow, river, backwaters") in support of the point. The peasant poets had creatively combined Aleksey Koltsov and Blok, progressing from folk symbols to literary symbols, although Esenin was more nearly a combination of Koltsov and Bely, especially the Bely of *Zoloto v lazuri* (*Gold in Azure*).[45]

Lvov-Rogachevsky actually severed Esenin from the nineteenth century tradition of Russian peasant poetry, and described the work of young contemporary peasant poets as suggestive and melodious, one that infected the reader with the music of their moods, a poetry at once nebulous, liquid, and diffuse. Their poems were shadows, their images symbols.[46] Through their folk connection the peasant poets found national roots, but in their creative method they were Symbolists.[47]

In speaking of "Marfa the Mayoress," "Cossack Us," "The Comrade," "Otherworldly Call," and "Otchar'," Lvov-Rogachevsky described Esenin as a peasant poet whose every line burned with the fires of rapture and dream, with the exultation characteristic of Easter songs. His poetry transmitted the melodious calls of Russia on the rampage (*buistvennaia Rus'*). The poems, he wrote, were the product of an enraptured mood rather than a profound revolutionary world view. Esenin had tried to "wed the religious to the revolutionary." But inspired only by the elemental protest of a popular uprising as he was, he had no revolutionary social content. Like all peasant poets, he accepted the revolution, but again like them, he suffered from the "disease of paying allegiance to two faiths."[48]

Distinguishing between Esenin and the Imaginists, in 1921 Lvov-Rogachevsky wrote that Esenin's Symbolism had nothing whatever in common with the Marinetti-type Futurism of the Imaginists. Lvov-Rogachevsky took both Mariengof and Shershenevich to task for their inorganic combinations of unreal, narcotic dream images. They violated the law of organic poetic unity, he said, eliminated verbal meaning and so deprived poetry of content. Art was severed from life, poetic creativity snuffed out, and the road to self-knowledge closed. Mariengof's and Shershenevich's putrescent poetry was the product of sick, ravaged, amoral souls. Their search for unusual and new combinations of images was joined with a cultivation of the disgusting. Mariengof's poems in particular were death-oriented, blasphemous, suicidal, and psychotic.[49] Lvov-Rogachevsky decided that Esenin's Imaginism was more of a pose and gesture than a characteristic trait. If anything, his Symbolism was close to the psychological parallelism typical of that patriarchal peasant view of the world that lent profound meaning to his images.[50]

In a speech in memory of Esenin delivered at the State Academy for Literary Studies on January 15, 1926, and never published, Lvov-Rogachevsky declared that Esenin had incorporated in his art all the acuteness of the contradictory character of a crisis-ridden (*perelomnyi*) epoch. The inner discord expressed in his poetry was the same discord found in the hearts of hundreds of thousands of his contemporaries, who had wept over his poems. All his poetry was dedicated to the homeless and the rakes; in particular his long poems "Pugachev," "Anna Snegina," and "The Black Man" described a homeless Russia, her vagabonds and wanderers.

To be sure, Esenin had shifted his poetic ground. In 1923 Esenin, Lvov-Rogachevsky thought, had begun to leave his Imaginist phase (he criticized "Pugachev" for longwindedness and monotony). He went to the Caucasus to escape his *Tavern Moscow* days, and came under Pushkin's influence in 1923–1925. His last period had been his most fertile one. He had tried to explain himself to others in such poems of 1924 as "Letter to Mother" and "Letter to a Woman," and he gave his songs to the mighty revolution in "Stanzas," "Lenin," "Poem about the Thirty-Six," "The Ballad about the Twenty-Six," and "The Song of the Great Campaign," all written in 1924. In his poem "Soviet *Rus'*" he had actually become a Soviet satellite (*sputnik*), Lvov-Rogachevsky declared.

But sadness and anxiety (*toska*) had infected Esenin's poetic development since about 1915. This had proved a powerful force, bringing with it a tenacious obsession with death and an accompanying sense of doom. Esenin's tragedy, Lvov-Rogachevsky said, lay in his inability to break with his forefathers and place his whole trust in the new Russia, brimming with energies.[51]

The critic Georgy Yakubovsky (1891–1930) belonged to the

Smithy group of proletarian writers (*Kuznitsa*). The Smithys rejected any artistic expression of extreme individualism, as they called it, whether of the moribund Symbolist, Futurist, or Imaginist currents in Russian literature. They preached a collective proletarian consciousness in art, artistic dynamism, and revolutionary Romanticism.[52]

But the Smithy's theory of aesthetics—and Yakubovsky's in particular—went beyond the typical Marxist confines of literary criticism. Its theory of art incorporated an almost mystical and intuitive sense of reality. Examples of this were the group's Romantic view of man's capacity to emulate the strength of metals; its belief in the boundless power of man's genius;[53] its lyrical flights of fancy about a universal art expressing the beauty of existence;[54] its feelings of spiritual kinship with past human creative experience; and its almost cosmic sense of solidarity with life and being, as if the entire universe were on their side.[55]

When Yakubovsky wrote of Esenin in 1926, his theoretical links with the Smithy groups—which had reached its apogee in 1921-1922—were still in evidence. He displayed a very high regard for the gift of lyrical poetry—in his view the quintessence of poetic speech was granted only by nature herself.[56] He had a pronouncedly mystical intuitive sense of being as poetic material: he believed that, somewhere at the heart of existence, always beckoning to the creative artist but always just beyond reach, one could find the objective truth of life. This conception, strongly reminiscent of the Symbolist poetic sensibility (particularly Blok's), could not, to Yakubovsky's mind, be entirely derived from historical and social economic forces and Marxist class consciousness.[57] Yakubovsky almost seems to have been a poetic spirit functioning in a critical capacity.

In 1926, Yakubovsky wrote of the lyrical freshness and spontaneity of Esenin's poetry, qualities which, he thought, made him a spiritual heir of Blok. Of course Blok had been a lyrical philosopher-poet, while Esenin was only a potentially morbid lyrical bard by comparison, but still, Esenin continued Blok's work.[58]

Like other Marxists of the time, Yakubovsky did discern a creative shift in Esenin's poetic focus in 1924. He considered "The Song of the Great Campaign" a step toward the revolution; hence, he said, Esenin should be evaluated not only in terms of what he had given, but also in terms of what he, like others in the same position, *"might have given"* (Yakubovsky's italics).[59]

V *Esenin and Gorbachev*

Although not so narrow minded as, say, the Octobrist critic Lelevich, Georgy Gorbachev (1897–1942) felt that literature should definitely be under the control of politically responsible bodies, and not nonparty literary organizations.[60]

In a book published in 1927, Gorbachev devoted a few very interesting pages to Esenin. Esenin, in his view, was a neo-peasant poet whose talent had flowered with the coming of the revolution. His embryonic beginnings, however, had to be sought in the prewar period.

A typical half-intellectual with little education and culture, Esenin was socially linked to the well-to-do peasantry, the class influenced both by bookish learning and to a certain degree by the spiritual current of sectarianism, so that it held itself aloof from the peasant masses. Esenin's prerevolutionary idyllic depiction of the village was the outcome of these social influences, as was his mystic and aesthetic, Symbolist acceptance of the October revolution. He experienced the revolution at times as a religious revelation, at times as an antireligious rebellion. But his religiousness did not express the way of life, the beliefs and social sympathies of the Russian peasantry in general. Consequently, such images as his beggar Christ were taken from Russian legends, which gave his poetry of 1912–1916 a humble, gentle, and "mistily passive" tone of the sort found in Blok's early poetry.

Gorbachev stressed Esenin's poetic links with Blok. Esenin, he wrote, exhibited a mystical sense like Blok's. Even in 1918–1919, while under the influence of Scythian ideas, he followed Blok by seeing the revolution in mystic and cosmic terms. And his early poetry—though a stylized imitation of folk art and clearly linked to the folk song—was even more powerfully influenced by Blok's *Poems to the Beautiful Lady*. In fact, the essential characteristic of all Esenin's poems from beginning to end was a melodiousness (*napevnost'*) that brought him still closer to Blok.

Of Imaginism Gorbachev had nothing good to say. He thought the movement a mere vulgarization of Futurism without any independent values. The movement offered a cynical, bohemian escape from moral, ideological, and social responsibilities.

In his last period—beginning with the *Tavern Moscow* poems, essentially a lyrical diary—Esenin still harked back to Blok's songs. His own poems were more primitive than Blok's in their imagery, composition, and lexical content, but their autobiographical quality made them popular with the reader, who took them as intimate documents rather than literary fact. Gorbachev regarded *Tavern Moscow* as profoundly decadent in spirit, imbued with individualistic and antisocial moods.

Gorbachev commented on Esenin's misguided, idealist belief in the powers of the Russian peasantry, and suggested that in "Pugachev" Esenin had abandoned any hope of seeing the peasantry achieve its revolution independently.

The social significance of the *Tavern Moscow* poems, on the other hand, lay in the "helplessly savage protest of the heir of decadent Symbolist poetry and of the declassed *kulak* progeny upon seeing the ruin of his traditional world." Yet, after demonstrating Esenin's ideological and literary bankruptcy, Gorbachev claimed that Esenin had nonetheless in his last period become a proletarian Fellow Traveler.[61]

CHAPTER 11

Esenin and Eseninism

I Eseninism as a Social Evil

IN the wake of Esenin's suicide in December of 1925 there arose something disparagingly called *Eseninshchina*, or Eseninism. Eseninism marked the beginning of Esenin's fall into official disrepute.

Eseninism was associated with a contagious suicidal state of mind that triggered, it was held, a wave of suicides. The extent of this disturbing social phenomenon is difficult to gauge, and proved a sensitive area of investigation during my stay in the Soviet Union in 1964–1965. We know from available material, however, that hostile critics often laid the blame for these suicides either directly on Esenin, on his decision to commit suicide and his emotionally charged poetry, or, by implication, blamed his suicide and its social consequences on his broken state of health, his philistine bourgeois environment, and his bohemian way of life, including the "friends" he kept, usually identified as various hues of Imaginists.[1] But, as Gleb Struve has pointed out, suicides were a frequent occurrence at that time, when disillusionment with the revolution had reached a culmination after the introduction of the New Economic Policy, which was regarded by many as a step backward toward capitalism.[2] Hence Eseninism must be viewed as only one factor among many that aggravated the general social situation.

The Communist authorities worried about this disillusioned and defeatist attitude toward life, which clashed with the official Marxist optimism, and tried to neutralize it. As late as 1929 or 1930, however, Eseninism as a social ailment seemed far from eliminated.[3]

To counteract the destructive influence of Eseninism, Nikolay Semashko (1874–   ), people's commissar for health, felt compelled to comment on Esenin and his death. In an article that clearly reflected his apprehension over the outbreak and spread of suicides, especially among groups oriented toward the revolution, he admitted that contemporary life—with its nervous tensions, its growing complexity, its far from normal sexual and marital relationships and difficulties—did indeed provide fertile ground for nervous breakdowns that could lead to suicide. But, he added, one should not exaggerate the danger.

Esenin, he remarked, had been a victim of mental disorders in general, and of a lack of will power in particular. All his latest work demonstrated that he had lost his link with life. And the main cause of suicide was disillusionment and the loss of faith in life. These traits, he said, were characteristic of the intelligentsia, but not of the worker and peasant. It was therefore improbable that mass suicide threatened the proletarian and peasant youth of the country. The best way to fight disillusionment was to correct the social conditions that gave rise to it. Furthermore, friendly attention toward psychologically vacillating (*nervno-neustoichivyi*) individuals might be a beginning in the fight against suicide, a battle that in the end would accelerate socialist construction.[4]

Semashko's fears prompted him to write yet a second article on the subject, in which he advocated a "keep yourself busy" type of cure. A heightened social consciousness, an interest in work, and a collective sense of involvement, he said, might help in reducing the number of suicides, still very great. This would prevent, he hoped, those nervous disorders that were a legacy from the old capitalist system. Small wonder that the declassed and disillusioned bourgeois Esenin had taken his life. But Soviet society, in Semashko's estimation, provided no grounds for suicide, and, though the young should be protected, the Russian intelligentsia, workers, and peasants would not become infected by the suicidal germ.[5]

Available information makes it appear that the overall situation at the time was much more alarming than Semashko would have us believe. The proletarian playwright Nikolay Pogodin (1900–   ), for instance, wrote of a school in the town of Eysk, where the students had fallen prey to a dangerous and decadent mood after Esenin's suicide, and one schoolgirl had been strangled at her own request. The trial of the boy who had accommodated her revealed that the mood among the students at the school was one of emptiness and premonition of death. Esenin's suicide poem, written in his own blood, had become for them a biblical commandment, and he himself a teacher of a new philosophy of "life" that had stimulated many a group discussion on suicide there. The victim, who had once before attempted suicide, had herself written poetry about the precariousness of life—but her teachers praised her instead of reproving her. Such occurrences, Pogodin concluded, justified a social purge in that school.[6]

Vladimir Gilyarovsky, a psychiatrist at Moscow State University No. 2, tried to show that Esenin's suicide was not symptomatic of the times, and that the proper ideological upbringing of the young would avert suicide in general.[7] But as late as 1929 G. Pokrovsky recalled that—very shortly after Esenin's death—the writer Andrey Sobol had taken his own life, and that there had in fact been a whole series of suicides among the students at the Higher Artistic-Theatrical Studios (*Vkhutemas*) in Moscow in the wake of Esenin's death.[8]

II *The Marxist Defense of Esenin*

In the initial stage of Eseninism, during 1926 and 1927, critical opinion of Esenin and his work followed one of two clear lines: the first criticized Esenin as a direct cause of Eseninism and associated him with it (e.g., the Futurist Kruchenykh and the proletarian militants); the second was critical of Eseninism, but dissociated the poet from it (e.g., most Marxists and, among the Futurists, Mayakovsky).

It is an ironic fact of the history of literary criticism in the 1920s that, during the posthumous abuse of Esenin, it was for the most part Marxist critics of standing who rallied to his moral defense by dissociating him from Eseninism. In a sense their defense, quite apart from personal sympathy or conviction, or possible considerations of political self-interest, may also have been prompted by guilt feelings, which marked many of the obituaries of Esenin at the time. This feeling of common guilt emerges clearly in the short speech given by the former Smithy poet Vladimir Kirillov (1899–   ), chairman of the union of poets (*Soiuz poetov*), on December 31, 1925, during Esenin's funeral:

Comrades! Today our literary family is experiencing a great sorrow. One of the best poets, one of those who had after Koltsov and Pushkin managed most talentedly, sensitively and thoughtfully to feel and transmit to us the mood of the village, to convey to us the poetry of its fields and forests, has gone away from us forever. The tragic death of the poet must move us to reflect deeply over our literary life. Let us then, comrades, make a vow over this fresh grave to change some of the negative aspects of this life, and together to create that friendly, comradely atmosphere which will make such deaths as Esenin's impossible.[9]

In his *Pravda* article of 1926, Trotsky had expressed the hope that no notes of decadence would mar Esenin's memory.[10] Voronsky also attempted to rehabilitate Esenin morally in the eyes of contemporary officialdom and society. He admitted that Esenin was not a contemporary peasant poet, but argued that he could be of service to the state since his poetry bared the psychological "wounds of the contemporary way of life" (*rany nashego byta*). Nor was the Soviet Communist government to blame for his demise. It was true, Voronsky wrote, that there was no dearth of Marxist critics who expected a poet to versify on the subject of the latest burning editorial issues without any regard for his creative needs. But the actual literary policy of the Communist party, he explained, was far removed from such primitive vulgarization. The Soviet regime had at no time sought to constrict Esenin's creative impulses. On the contrary, Esenin had enjoyed exceptional regard, love, and esteem in official circles, which, indeed, had treated him with more care than he had ever lavished on himself. Voronsky denied that Esenin's as yet unpublished literary estate had been subjected to any political censorship. Esenin, he said, should have given more to the new Soviet world. But if anything was to blame for his end, it was the epoch, the spirit of the times. Who, he asked, would cast the first stone though? Who could deny that the tractor had after all as much historical right to exist as Esenin's handsome foal?[11]

Esenin's tragic suicide, Voronsky went on, exposed the necessity for a moral purge among Soviet Russia's stricken colony
of writers:

It is time that we eliminated sick and morbid manifestations among
our writers, in a consistent, firm and determined way and manner.
The representatives of Soviet power and of our party who influence
literary reality should take into account and understand the peculiarities of this environment, the distinctive characteristics of creative
work, the difficulties obstructing the way, but above all else, our
own writers should themselves tackle the problem of remedying the
situation and of improving their state of health.[12]

Karl Radek (1885–1939), a member of Trotsky's opposition
group,[13] wrote two articles on Esenin and Eseninism. His
analysis of Esenin also gave Radek an opportunity to comment
on the contemporary social and literary situation. In his first
article he described Esenin as one who had sung like a bird,
had had no social links, had pursued women and enjoyed life
until he tired of it all and ended his existence. Many contemporary writers were in the same predicament. But an artist, he
warned, could no longer afford to be a mere observer. Literature
should reflect life in its meaningful essence. There were Soviet
writers who had no real faith in the revolution and therefore
could not create. They were writers of the senses rather than
of thought.

Radek wrote that Esenin's tragedy was a "symptom of an
ailment in contemporary literature" (*simptom neduga literatury*).
A Soviet writer could overcome this ailment only by moving
toward communism through participation in social life. Those
who would not become convinced Communists would not become Soviet writers. Becoming a Communist was a matter of
life or death for Soviet writers, as Esenin's suicide proved.[14]

In his second article Radek spoke of a number of suicides
among members of the Komsomol, or Communist Youth Or-
ganization. He admitted that Esenin's poetic moods were frequently communicated to Soviet young people, who read his
poems with great delight. But it was a pity to blame Esenin's
poetry for the general problem of suicide. True, his lyrical
poetry was more communicative than proletarian poetry, which

just drummed away at its message; it appealed to his young readers because he was just as full of contradictions and confusion as they. Yet, in order to eliminate unhealthy tendencies among Soviet youth, it was not Esenin who should be fought, but the social causes behind such morbid phenomena. His poetry should not be used to conceal the real reasons for the suicides.

Radek blamed social conditions for the suicides. The poor and middle peasantry among the Komsomol youth, he pointed out, were deeply disoriented by the process of rural social disintegration and did not always understand the party's policies. These strata of the peasantry were always dissatisfied because they could not move to the city, the promised land of bread and a better life. The young proletarians who were members of Komsomol organizations found the factories also disillusioning. Esenin very much resembled these thousands of petty bourgeois Komsomol members, students and workers, who were not at all made of iron, as Komsomol poetry pictured them. This petty bourgeois youth reflected the vacillations of the peasant masses and the urban poor. They exhibited an innate distrust in the socialist character of Russia's development.

Radek urged that decadence (*upadochnichesvto*) among youth be fought by improving its material conditions of life and by training it ideologically for world revolution. Esenin's poetry was but a thermometer, indicating ill health. It was pointless to blame the thermometer for gauging the fever; instead the sickness itself should be cured.[15]

Anatoly Lunacharsky (1875–1933), commissar for education, warned that Esenin and Eseninism should not be equated. Esenin was a poet of very delicate sensibility, and quite responsive to his environment. To see him only as hooligan, pessimist, and decadent was too one-sided, and of little benefit to Marxists. In fact, in taking his own life Esenin had morally rehabilitated himself.[16]

Yakubovsky argued that since it was natural for lyric poetry to express the dynamism of life, lyric poets could not help being inspired by the revolution. One could not deny the revolution its lyricism, and he felt Esenin had contributed to that.[17]

Finally, Gorbachev agreed that some negative elements of society had found justification for their pessimism and hooliganism in Esenin's *Moscow Tavern* poems. In this sense Esenin's poems were dangerous because they disoriented the psyche of unstable readers. But if one took Esenin—that peasant idealist lost in a proletarian world—and his work as a whole, and explained it properly, then it had original literary and cultural values to offer.[18]

III *The Futurists: Kruchenykh and Mayakovsky*

Among the Fellow Travelers, the Futurists (especially Kruchenykh) were most hostile to Esenin and/or Eseninism during this period of posthumous defamation.

Kruchenykh helped wield the official cudgel against Esenin as progenitor of Eseninism. Esenin's poetry was harmful, he wrote, and the suicidal temptations of Eseninism could only be resisted through effective literary groupings that would redirect the energies of writers under Eseninist influence toward the more organized world of Soviet literature. These words, incidentally, clashed strangely with Kruchenykh's belief that poetic destiny was always independent of a poet's times.[19]

Another of Kruchenykh's "productions" dealt solely with the problem of Eseninism. Kruchenykh was taken aback by the fact that other critics had failed to give proper recognition to his fight against Eseninism. He contrasted LEF's revolutionary, constructive essence to the Imaginists' hooliganism and romanticization of taverns, suggesting Futurism as a healthy antidote to those who still idolized Esenin. He also endorsed Mayakovsky's poetic retaliation against Esenin's suicide.[20]

In his essay "How to Make Poetry," Mayakovsky revealed that his poetic reaction to Esenin's suicide had been triggered by an urgent official directive to the poets of the USSR to write on Esenin. He estimated that 99 percent of the poems and articles published on Esenin's death were harmful, empty, insincere pamphleteering nonsense. In Mayakovsky's words, Esenin's suicide poem was beginning to exert a "swift and unfailing" effect, and Kruchenykh's "rancid" little books did little to combat it.[21]

Mayakovsky also participated in debates on Eseninism on February 13 and March 5, 1927. In the first debate, he said that it was meaningless to equate the problem of Eseninism simply with Esenin. In his travels across the Soviet Union, Mayakovsky went on, he had found that some 35–40 percent of poets belonging to proletarian literary organizations were under Esenin's poetic influence. But this was largely due to their lack of literary culture, which caused them to exaggerate Esenin's poetic stature: they did not truly understand him, and, carried away by the power of his lyricism, they did not realize that his poetry was an escape from reality. Mayakovsky reminded his audience that poetry was a weapon in the interests of the proletarian revolution, and that Esenin's art, being without use to the revolution, amounted to nothing. The real task in investigating Eseninism was to discover the poetic secret of such spiritual penetration. Mayakovsky ended by pointing out that Esenin's hooliganism in Soviet society could perhaps be of use to the revolution; but that Eseninism was a disgraceful thing they themselves had invented.[22]

During the second debate Mayakovsky focused on Eseninism as a far more terrifying phenomenon than Esenin himself, stressing the fact that Esenin could not be blamed for the spread of Eseninism, the creation of his followers.[23]

CHAPTER 12

Conclusion

IN Chapter 8 I suggested that Esenin's poetic predicament in the early years of the Soviet era stemmed from the Romantic nature of his poetic vision. In this sense his creative dilemma was not *ultimately* a result of social, or even political, circumstances—although they did aggravate his poetic condition—but was caused by the "inner forms" of his poetic imagination. I have tried to demonstrate that the creative energy of his poetic vision was generated by two innate and opposing forces: one dynamic and visionary, constructive and liberating, essentially socially oriented, idealistically directed toward the future and therefore personally centrifugal; the other—which in the end proved to be the more powerful of the two—static and oppressive, a self-destructive and centripetal force, tending toward final dissolution.

These two dialectical streams of poetic consciousness in Esenin, genetically and psychically determined, were undoubtedly shaped by his experiences in the countryside and by his folk and Symbolist sources of inspiration. In fact it was probably Symbolism—with its emphasis upon poetry as a free spiritual force bringing transcendental knowledge, and the poet as a unique carrier of such poetic impulse—that enabled Esenin to shape his poetic imagery in terms of a utopian and equally Romantic vision of a Russian peasant paradise on earth. It was, however, these streams of consciousness taken together that engendered the poetic tension of Esenin's lyrical energy. He said as much metaphorically when, in a poem of 1925, he asked his sweetheart to light a fire in the stove and make the bed for the night: without her, the snowstorm within him would rage on without stopping (III, 106). Without her, in other words, without his beloved, without the warming energy of a utopian "life" vision, he would succumb to the cold force of "death" within.

162

These were the spiritual coordinates of his poetic vision. In interpreting his poetic work at the time (in the first decade after 1917), however, few critics tried to define the nature of Esenin's poetic perception in more than general terms. The reason for this lay in the extremely political and ideological temper of the age. Critics were less interested in an "objective" poetic analysis of his work than in a subjective, ideological interpretation of it. As a result, critics did not allow the poetic material to shape their interpretations, but sought to shape the material through their interpretations. Instead of a relatively free and imaginative interplay between material and critic, a contest ensued between the poetic vision and its interpretation, between the inner laws and forces motivating Esenin's poetic drive for creative self-expression and the extraliterary, prescriptive, or pragmatic ends of Marxists and non-Marxists alike.

It is intriguing to reflect on the predominantly utilitarian character of the critical response to Esenin (except for the "academic" critics Kravtsov and Neyman perhaps), and to speculate on the extent to which such a "critical" attitude in the field of letters was either the direct or indirect outcome of a politically triumphant Marxism. In any case, there appeared very little purely aesthetic criticism of Esenin's poetic work (even the Formalists had their partisan motivations), a fact that recalls Boris Eichenbaum's observation of 1925 that the turning away from normative aesthetics was more or less typical for the whole of the contemporary science of art.[1]

In this struggle, motives of a personal, intuitive, and poetic nature clashed with the extraliterary cerebrations of critics. It was characteristic that Marxist criticism should have dwelt, not on the nature of Esenin's poetic imagination—which should be the basic concern of literary criticism—but focused instead on his "poetic" dilemma, that is, his inability to dedicate himself wholly to a political revolution from whose cold and calculated demands he was poetically estranged. His poetic predicament was thus defined, not in creative, but in political and social terms, a sociological operation of which not only Marxist critics were guilty. In this connection, one may add that the campaign against Eseninism only indicated that purely political, social, and moral criteria had by then gained the upper hand in the field of art. To a degree Fellow Traveler criticism was also marred by ideological, social, or purely partisan considerations. This was as true, to take a few examples, of Ivanov-Razumnik's and Klyuev's critical views as it was of the very partial Imaginist, Futurist, and even Formalist positions. Admittedly, literary criticism is by nature interpretative, yet most Esenin criticism of the time lacked that more objective quality that characterized both Kravtsov's and Neyman's findings (at least their disagreements remained within aesthetic bounds). In this critical process taken as a whole, the contours of Esenin's poetic vision were lost sight of, even though some critics (e.g., Klyuev, Shklovsky, Tynyanov, Kruchenykh, Voronsky, Trotsky, and Gorbachev) did make an occasional aesthetically relevant foray into Esenin's psychology.

Yet in retrospect at least, one may also discover the existential coordinates of his poetic vision by plotting the path of his creative development in autobiography, that is, by simply following his poetic direction in a world that was not sympathetic to the lyrical spirit, as Trotsky knew.

Let us digress briefly. It would not be difficult to show that—in Cleanth Brooks' terminology—the "paradoxical" nature of lyric poetry as a genre (Esenin's two dialectical streams of poetic consciousness would support the point)—and, one might add, in this lies the never-ending source of its Romanticism—has been less at home with explicit social or political subjects than with imagery per se (imagism, folklore), motifs of introspection (inspired subjectivity), suggestive pastoral motifs (nature), temporal but not always historically factual stimuli (especially the past and the future), transcendental motifs (Symbolism), themes of life and love and alienation, disillusionment, decline and death (the tragic sense).

It is these modes of the lyrical spirit—and not political or utilitarian categories—in which Esenin's poetic art is cast. In fact, his thematics not only characterize his poetic work, but also explain to a very considerable extent his creative autobiography. That is the existential thread marking the true course along which his poetic vision developed: his attraction to Blok and Bely (inspired subjectivity, Symbolism); his hostility to Mayakovsky and the proletarians (the pastoral sensibility); his attraction to Klyuev (the patriarchal past, folklore); his gravitation toward Ivanov-Razumnik and the initial, "idealist" stages of the revolution (the dream of a peasant utopia, in itself a transposition of the Romantic impulse to "social" ends); his attraction to the Imaginists and later to Pushkin (aesthetics per se coupled with a sense of poetic election); Isadora Duncan and the West (the search for poetic acclaim and affirmation); his involvement with women ("love" as a source of poetic material); his *Tavern Moscow* phase (life's disillusionment and ensuing alienation); and his testament "The Black Man" (dissolution and death).

Hence there was a natural logic to Esenin's poetic development, for both his life and his work were molded by the creative requirements of his poetic imagination. As Esenin said on several occasions, all he really wanted was to be left alone as a poet. Literary criticism had, of course, its function as a means of poetic recognition, and his popularity with contemporary audiences and readers was a measure of his success as a poet. But one can readily understand the lyric poet's profound distaste at being labeled, his dislike of any critical dismemberment of his own work, whether in the interests of the revolution or of any other self-proclaimed ideology or poetic school. The Fellow Traveler Fedor Zhits (1892–   ) was right in declaring that it was pointless to fit Esenin into some *a priori* formula. Instead, like Susan Sontag in more recent times, he in effect suggested that one would come closer to the nerve center of Esenin's poetry if one moved as far as possible away from interpretation and let Esenin's work speak for itself. In the process, what the reader found, Zhits explained—especially in Esenin's more mature work—was a tragic sense of reality that spoke eloquently to the disillusioning social experiences of his contemporaries and ensured his lasting success. Writing more as reader than critic, and with the Marxist strictures upon the poet in mind, Zhits defended the Romantic poet in revolutionary society:

I vote with both hands for a cheerful mood in life and art. But at the same time . . . , I should like with all my heart to leave a place in art for tragic motifs. For the prime sources of such art well forth

from pain and dissatisfaction, not from joy and satiation. Poets are
the heralds of the eternal and restless quest of mankind, and genuine
art is more often a deviation from life's norm than a positive illus-
tration of reality. The motifs of mutinous pain vary, but the artist
is by his very nature a rebel, an "oppositionist." In the machine
age, the poet exalts the coach, in the infancy stage of peoples he
extols iron and concrete. . . . This does not mean, however, that
the tragic motifs of art infect life with pessimism. According to the
law of inverse reflexion which often regulates art, pain gives birth
to energy for struggle and manliness, the dissonant notes of the
poet help one find the resultant mean of the dream and the fact of
being, of complexity and simplicity.[2]

Esenin's poetic vision as the integral of his life and art, the
unity between the lyrical motifs of his work and the important
personal "poetic" events of his life, bring to mind the scattered
remarks—intuitively correct, but too general to be of any
critical use—to the effect that Esenin's life and poetry were
indeed inextricably linked. Esenin's attempt to come to terms
with Marxism (especially his relationship with Voronsky), was
but an act of expediency, a desperate try to sustain himself
poetically in an unfavorable environment. Ivan Rozanov was
right when he maintained that:

It is not only the environment but also the spirit of the times which
influences the achievement of poetry and the development of talents.
The fire of poetry does not always burn with an even flame: sometimes it grows weaker, sometimes it flares up and burns brighter than
before. The predominant currents, the surrounding atmosphere may
fan the poetic spark into a flame, but they may also extinguish it.[3]

Esenin's poetic failure was not due merely to his natural incapacity for artistic compromise, or to the unrealistic appraisal
of his position as a lyric poet in a proletarian-oriented Marxist
world, with all its accompanying creative aggravations, but
was ultimately caused by the "inner discord" of two mutually
exclusive streams of poetic consciousness, a fatal inner friction
whose first harbingers were signs of mounting poetic impotence.

Esenin, that "Don Quixote of the village," as Shershenevich
called him, whose Muse encountered a stirring emotional response among the reading public of his day and later, could

not simultaneously fend off his inner spiritual and an outer historical upheaval, was unable to survive the two-pronged offensive mounted against him by the inner events of his poetic being and the sociopolitical realities of the outside world. But the bitter experience he encountered on the road between his vision and its interpretation was incorporated in a poetry that has found its readers across all political barriers. In this, Esenin belongs to that distinguished fellowship of poets whose work testifies to the indomitable creative spirit of man.

ABBREVIATIONS USED IN THE NOTES AND REFERENCES

Esenin: E. F. Nikitina, ed. *Esenin, zhizn', lichnost', tvorchestvo.* Moscow: Izd-vo "Rabotnik prosveshcheniia," 1926.

Pamiati Esenina: *Pamiati Esenina: Sbornik statei.* Moscow: Vserossiiskii soyuz poetov, 1926.

Sergey Alexandrovich Esenin: Ivan Evdokimov, ed. *Sergey Alexandrovich Esenin. Vospominaniia: Sbornik statei.* Moscow-Leningrad: Gosizdat, 1926.

Sbornik: Yu. L. Prokushev, ed. *Sbornik: Vospominaniia o Sergee Esenine.* Moscow: Moskovskii rabochii, 1965

Ot simvolizma do Oktiabria: N. L. Brodsky and N. P. Siderov, eds. *Ot simvolizma do Oktiabria: Literaturnye manifesty.* Moscow: "Novaia Moskva," 1924. The Moscow 1929 edition is edited by N. L. Brodsky, Lvov-Rogachevsky and N. P. Sidorov and is entitled *Literaturnye manifesty: ot simvolizma k Oktiabriu.* Moscow: Federatsiia, 1929 (See p. 179n95; also p. 183n36).

IMLI: Institut mirovoi literatury, Moscow.

Notes and References

Preface

1. There is little that is new in the first four volumes of the later edition. It offers no new significant poems apart from sixteen from his earliest 1910–1912 manuscripts, three of 1915, and one of 1925. Of these, all but two (1915, 1925) appear as a supplement to volume five (pp. 201–11). The fifth volume does contain twenty-two new letters, but here too there is no material that would provide us with new insights into Esenin and his work. An exception may be one or two instances that might possibly shed additional light on Esenin's "Persian" experience (pp. 49, 137, 299–300). There is also a new reference by Esenin to one of Alexander Blok's poems (p. 71).

Chapter One

1. Alexandra Esenina, "Eto vse mne rodnoe i blizkoe. O Sergee Esenine," *Molodaia gvardiia*, 7 (1960), 215.
2. Sobranie sochinenii (Moscow: Goslitizdat, 1961–62), V, 16.
3. V, 11, 15, 24.
4. V, 16.
5. Esenina, p. 218.
6. V, 8.
7. E. M. Khitrov, "V Spas-Klepikovskoi shkole," *Sbornik*, pp. 83–85.
8. V, 24, 8–9.
9. V, 16.
10. Khitrov, pp. 84, 86.
11. Esenina, "Eto vse mne rodnoe i blizkoe. O Sergee Esenine," *Molodaia gvardiia*, 8 (1960), 209.
12. A. R. Izryadnova, "Vospominaniia," *Sbornik*, pp. 100–101.
13. N. A. Sardanovsky, "Iz moikh vospominanii o Sergee Esenine" (1926), *IMLI*, F. 32, Op. 3, No. 36, p. 5. See I, 60.
14. Ryurik Ivnev, "Ob Esenine," *Sergey Alexandrovich Esenin*, p. 10.
15. N. N. Livkin, "V Mlechnom puti," *Sbornik*, p. 117.
16. Ibid.
17. V, 9.

18. Alexander Blok, *Sobranie sochinenii*, 8 vols. (Moscow-Leningrad: Goslitizdat, 1960–1963), VIII, 441.

19. Blok, VIII, 444–45.

20. V, 12. See also pp. 270, 274.

21. Sergey Gorodetsky, "O Sergee Esenine. Vospominaniia," *Novyi mir*, 2 (1926), 139–40. See also Part II, Chapter 9 of this study.

22. V, 117.

23. Yu. D. Loman, "Fedorovsky Gorodok," *Sbornik*, pp. 161–65.

24. See Vadim Shershenevich, "Poet Sergey Esenin," *Zaria zapada*, January 15, 1926, p. 3.

25. P. Yushin, *Poeziia Sergeya Esenina, 1910–1923 godov* (Moscow: Izd-vo Moskovskogo Universiteta, 1966), pp. 166, 182, 28.

26. V, 13.

27. Shershenevich, p. 3.

28. V, 13.

29. V, 17.

30. V. L. Lvov-Rogachevsky, "Pamiati S. A. Esenina" (speech delivered in the Literary Section of the State Academy of Sciences, January 15, 1926), *IMLI*, F. 32, Op. 3, No. 22. Corrected typescript signed by the author.

31. The February revolution brought about the tsar's abdication and the formation of a provisional representative government. The second, or October, revolution of 1917 resulted in a Communist takeover. To 1918 Russia used the "old style" Julian Calendar as opposed to the "new style" Gregorian Calendar in use today.

32. Ivnev, pp. 17–18.

33. V, 13. Yushin suggests that Esenin's desertion took place sometime after March 20, 1917, as this was Esenin's last day in Tsarskoe Selo. See P. F. Yushkin, *Sergey Esenin. Ideino-tvorcheskaia evoliutsiia* (Moscow: Izd-vo Moskovskogo Universiteta, 1969), p. 197.

34. V, 17.

35. E. Naumov, *Sergey Esenin: zhizn' i tvorchestvo* (Leningrad: Uchpedgiz, 1960), p. 62.

36. V, 22.

37. Petr Oreshin, "Moe znakomstvo s Sergeem Eseninym (K godovshchine smerti. Vospominaniia)," *Krasnaia niva*, 52 (1926), 20, 19.

38. V. S. Chernyavsky, "Pervye shagi," *Sbornik*, p. 148.

Chapter Two

1. P. Sakulin, "Narodnyi zlatotsvet," *Vestnik Evropy*, 5 (1916), 204–207.

2. Page references to poems in this chapter come from vol. I of the 1961–1962 edition and are cited in the body of the text.

3. Stenka Razin was the great seventeenth century peasant revolutionary leader.

4. V, 22.

Chapter Three

1. V, 13. The Soviet government left for Moscow on March 10, in view of the fact that Petrograd was in danger from military attack by white forces.

2. Oreshin, p. 20.

3. V, 13. The manifesto was published on January 30, 1919.

4. V, 9.

5. Ivnev, pp. 21–22.

6. Ivan Startsev, "Moi vstrechi s Eseninym," *Sergey Alexandrovich Esenin*, pp. 62–64, 66–69, 73–75, 78, 79–80.

7. N. Poletaev, "Esenin za vosem' let," *Sergey Aleksandrovich Esenin*, pp. 103, 98–99, 101–102.

8. Georgy Ustinov, "Gody voskhoda i zakata: vospominaniia o Sergee Esenine," *Pamiati Esenina*, pp. 83–84. See also G. Ustinov, "Sergey Esenin i ego smert'," *Krasnaia gazeta*, December 29, 1925, p. 4. See further Esenin's application for membership in the Literary-Artistic Club of the Soviet Section of the Union of Writers, Painters and Poets, in the spring of 1919: V, 133–34.

9. Kirillov, pp. 173–74.

10. V, 18, 22.

11. M. D. Royzman, "Vospominaniia o Esenine," *IMLI*, F. 32, Op. 3, No. 33, corrected typescript, pp. 4–5.

12. In 1924 Esenin recollected that between 1918 and 1921 his roving life had taken him to Turkestan, the Caucasus, Persia, the Crimea, Bessarabia, the Orenburg steppes, the Murmansk littoral, Arkhangelsk and Solovki: V, 17–18. According to V. Volpin, Esenin's sojourn in Turkestan became the poetic inspiration behind "Pugachev" and *Persian Motifs.*

13. See D. Blagoy, "Materialy k kharakteristike Sergeya Esenina (Iz arkhiva poeta Shiryaevtsa)," *Krasnaia nov'*, 2 (1926), 203, who reproduces Esenin's letter with its original orthography.

14. V, 145, 147, 149.

15. Ivan Rozanov, "Moe znakomstvo s Eseninym," *Pamiati Esenina*, pp. 22, 23, 24, 35, 22.

16. Ibid., p. 20.

17. Kirillov, p. 173.

18. Semyon Fomin, "Iz vospominanii," *Pamiati Esenina*, p. 132.

19. V, 139. See also Anatolij Marienhof, "Roman ohne Luege," in Milo Dor and Reinhard Federman, eds., *Gemordete Literatur: Dichter der russischen Revolution* (Salzburg: Otto Müller Verlag, 1963), p. 97, who quotes almost the complete letter, but with variations from the Soviet edition.

20. V, 140.

Chapter Four

1. Page references to the poems and volume numbers are cited in the text.

2. See S. D. Labkovsky, *Poeziia prorokov* (Berlin-Petersburg-Moscow: Izd-vo Z. I. Grzhebina, 1923), pp. 41–46.

Chapter Five

1. Irma Duncan and Allan Ross Macdougall, *Isadora Duncan's Russian Days and Her Last Years in France* (New York: Covici-Friede, 1929), p. 85.

2. Ilya Ehrenburg, *Men, Years, Life: First Years of Revolution 1918–21* (London: MacGibbon & Kee, 1962), II, 161–62.

3. Gorodetsky, pp. 141–42.

4. Anatoly Mariengof, *Vospominanie o Esenine* (Moscow: Akts. Izd-vo O-vo "Ogonek," 1926), pp. 52–53.

5. M. Babenchikov, "Esenin," *Sergey Aleksandrovich Esenin*, pp. 43–44.

6. Startsev, p. 83.

7. Ibid., pp. 122, 124, 125, 126–27.

8. Ehrenburg, p. 165.

9. Duncan and Macdougall, p. 134.

10. V, 156.

11. Duncan and Macdougall, pp. 142–43.

12. Ibid., p. 165.

13. Ibid., p. 171.

14. Ibid., pp. 175–76, 178, 181–82, 185–86, 189.

15. V, 14.

16. A copy of the original letter was made on January 8, 1968, from Kusikov's private Esenin archives in Paris by Professor Gordon McVay, just before they disappeared under not so mysterious circumstances: see *Novyi zhurnal*, 95 (1969), 229.

17. Ibid., 230.

18. See V, 156–72. An eleventh letter, of an official nature and written from Duesseldorf (July 29, 1922) to the acting people's

commissar of external affairs, M. M. Litvinov, has been included in the latest (1966–1968) edition of Esenin's poems. Esenin's correspondence from abroad covers the period from June 1922 to the spring of 1923. There are no letters at all from the months between the spring of 1923 and December 19, 1923.

19. Ibid., pp. 158–60, 166–69.

20. Ibid., pp. 171–72. For Esenin's impressions of the U.S., see also his "Zheleznyi mirgorod" ("The Iron Town"), IV, 257–68, which appeared in *Izvestiia* on his return from abroad. Apart from a strategic need, no doubt, to ingratiate himself with the authorities, in this article he responded positively to the promising young genius of the American people, contrasting their potential with the spiritually limiting nature of their technological achievements. The latter impressed him, nonetheless, and made him think of the need to industrialize Russia also.

21. Duncan and Macdougall, pp. 198–222, 276–80.

22. Ivan Evdokimov, "Sergey Alexandrovich Esenin," *Sergey Alexandrovich Esenin*, p. 228.

23. Georgy Ustinov, "Moi vospominaniia ob Esenine," *Sergey Alexandrovich Esenin*, pp. 158–59.

24. A. Voronsky, "Pamiati o Esenine (iz vospominanii)," *Krasnaia nov'*, 2 (1926), 207.

25. Ibid., pp. 207–208.

26. Ibid., pp. 208–209.

27. Rozanov, p. 51.

28. Ivan Rakhillo, *Moskovskie vstrechi* (Moscow: Moskovskii rabochii, 1961), pp. 50, 55.

29. S. Maschan, "Iz arkhiva S. Esenina, materialy i soobshcheniia," *Novyi mir*, 12 (1959), 273.

30. Ustinov, "Gody voskhoda i zakata," p. 87.

31. N. Tikhonov, "Iz vstrech s Eseninym," *Krasnaia gazeta*, December 31, 1925, p. 5.

32. N. Aseev, "Tri vstrechi s Eseninym," *Sergey Alexandrovich Esenin*, p. 192.

33. Maschan, p. 273.

34. Ivan Gruzinov, "Esenin razgovarivaet o literature i iskusstve," *Segodnia*, 1 (1926), 85.

35. I. B. Galant, "O dushevnoi bolezni S. Esenina," in G. B. Segalik, ed., *Klinicheskii arkhiv genial'nosti i odarennosti (Evrapatologii)*, II, 2 (Sklad izdaniia "Prakticheskaia Meditsina," Leningrad, 1926), 115–32.

36. Ivnev, pp. 32–33.

37. Lev Fainshtein, "Sergey Esenin v Baku (1924–25)," *Sergey Alexandrovich Esenin*, pp. 121–23.

38. See Volf Erlikh, *Pravo na pesn'* (Leningrad: Izd-vo Pisatelei v Leningrade, 1930), pp. 76–77; and also Startsev, pp. 89–90.

39. Gorodetsky, p. 145. See also Blagoy, p. 200.

40. Startsev, p. 87.

41. See G. A. Benislavskaya, Predsmertnaia zapiska, December 3, 1926, *IMLI*, F. 32, Op. 5, No. 16. Photocopy.

42. See *Zapiski Benislavskoy, G.A. 1921, 1923, IMLI*, F. 32, Op. 5, No. 6. Photocopy.

43. Sofya Vinogradskaya, *Kak zhil Sergey Esenin* (Moscow: Akts. Izd. o-vo "Ogonek," 1926), pp. 28–29, 31–33, 20–22, 25–27.

44. Vinogradskaya, pp. 28, 32, 14–15. Actually Esenin left Benislavskaya in June 1925, moved in with Tolstaya in July, and married her on September 18, 1925. See Erlikh, pp. 25–26. See also V, 380.

45. Erlikh, pp. 48, 57–58, 62, 75–77, 79–81.

46. Evdokimov, p. 215.

47. V. Nasedkin, *Poslednii god Esenina (Iz vospominanii)* (Moscow: "Nikitinskie Subbotniki," 1927), pp. 9, 11, 15, 17–21, 25–32, 37, 39–41, 43–46.

48. Startsev, p. 91.

49. V. Erlikh, "Chetyre dnia," *Pamiati Esenina*, p. 97; Erlikh, *Pravo na pesn'*, pp. 95–103.

50. E. Ustinova, "Chetyre dnia Sergeya Alexandrovicha Esenina," *Sergey Alexandrovich Esenin*, pp. 235–37.

51. Galant, pp. 129, 131–32.

52. Gorodetsky, p. 137.

Chapter Six

1. Of these, Esenin made four—including the poem "Wolf's End"—introductory to the cycle of nine "Tavern Moscow" poems proper written abroad. Seven made up the "Love of a Hooligan" group of poems, dedicated in the latter half of 1923 to the actress A. L. Miklashevskaya; they were followed by one concluding poem. Except for one work of 1921, the poems covered the period 1922–1923.

2. Page references to the poems and volume numbers are cited in the text.

3. See E. Naumov, *Sergey Esenin. Lichnost'. Tvorchestvo. Epokha* (Leningrad: Lenizdat, 1969), pp. 364–65.

Chapter Seven

1. Leon Shestov, *Chekhov and Other Essays*, New Introduction by

Sidney Monas (Ann Arbor: The University of Michigan Press, 1966), p. vii.

2. Ibid., p. 3.

3. The material for what follows is drawn in revised form from my article "Death and Decay: An Analysis of S. A. Esenin's Poetic Form," *Canadian Slavonic Papers*, X (Summer 1968), 180–209. For a more detailed lexical analysis, readers are referred to the same article. Page references to the poems and volume numbers are cited in the text.

Chapter Eight

1. Blok, VI, 115.

2. Osip Mandelshtam, *Sobranie sochinenii* (New York, 1955), p. 328.

3. *Yav'. Stikhi* (Moscow: Vtoraia Gosudarstvennaia tipografiia, 1919).

4. V. Pravdukhin, "Sergey Esenin," *Sibirskie ogni*, 1–2 (1926), 180.

Chapter Nine

1. V, 151.

2. Ivanov-Razumnik, *Russkaia literatura ot semidesiatykh godov do nashikh dnei*, 6th ed. (Berlin: Izd-vo "Skify," 1923), pp. 335–36, 340, 342, 344, 346, 348–49, 397.

3. Ivanov-Razumnik, *Pisatel'skie sud'by* (New York: Literaturnyi Fond, 1951), p. 3.

4. Ivanov-Razumnik, *Istoriia russkoi obshchestvennoi mysli*, 2 vols. (St. Petersburg: Tip. M. M. Stasiulevicha, 1908).

5. Ivanov-Razumnik, *Rossiia i Inoniia* (Berlin: Izd-vo "Skify," 1920), pp. 29–30, 7–8. See also his *Ispytanie v groze i bure* (Berlin: Izd-vo "Skify," 1920), pp. 12–13, 21, 37.

6. Ivanov-Razmunik, *Ispytanie v groze i bure*, pp. 40, 38, 37, 25, 26.

7. Ibid., pp. 21, 22, 27, 43–44.

8. Ivanov-Razumnik, "Sotsializm i revoliutsiia," *Skify*, 1 (1917), 306, 309 (also preface, xi).

9. Ivanov-Razumnik, "Poety i revoliutsiia," *Skify*, 2 (1918), 2, 5.

10. Ivanov-Razumnik, *Russkaia literatura ot semidesiatykh godov do nashikh dnei*, p. 383.

11. Ivanov-Razumnik, "Dve Rossii," *Skify*, 1 (1917), 214, 216, 218, 220, 224.

12. Ivanov-Razumnik, *Rossiia i Inoniia*, pp. 24, 20, 28, 26, 24.

13. Ippolit Udushev (pseudonym of Ivanov-Razumnik), "Vzgliad i nechto, otryvok (k stoletiiu 'Goria ot uma')," *Sovremennaia literatura: Sbornik statei* (Leningrad, 1925), pp. 171, 154–67, 178.

14. II, 37–38.

15. See Ponomareff, pp. 180–209.

16. V, 42–43.

17. V, 52.

18. V, 51.

19. V, 44, 54.

20. N. L. Leyzerov, in his article "Imazhinizm" (*Kratkaia literaturnaia entsiklopediia* [Moscow: Sovetskaia Entsiklopediia, 1966], III, 108) suggests that the movement may have dissolved as late as 1927.

21. See Anatoly Mariengof, *Buian-Ostrov: Imazhinizm* (Moscow: Kn-vo "Imazhinisty," 1920), pp. 18–19; V. Shershenevich, $2 \times 2 = 5$, *Listy imazhinista* (Moscow: Kn-vo "Imazhinisty," 1920), pp. 12–13; and Ivan Gruzinov, *Imazhinizma osnovnoe* (Moscow: Kn-vo "Imazhinisty," 1921), p. 13.

22. A. Mariengof and V. Shershenevich, "Sovremennye razmyshleniia," *Gostinitsa*, 4 (1924). No pagination was used by the journal.

23. See *Gostinitsa* 1 [3] (1924). See also A. Mariengof, "I v khvost i v grivu," *Gostinitsa* 2 (1923).

24. See "Deklaratsiia," V, 221, 222.

25. See "Pochti deklaratsiia" and "Vosem' punktov" in V, 227, 230, 231.

26. Gorodetsky, pp. 142–43, 137–38, 140–41.

27. Ivan Rozanov, "Esenin i ego sputniki," in *Esenin*, p. 84.

28. Ibid., pp. 87–88.

29. Rozanov, "Moe znakomstvo s Eseninym," pp. 39–40.

30. V, 237.

31. V, 55–61, esp. p. 56.

32. See C. V. Ponomareff, "The Image Seekers: An Analysis of Imaginist Poetic Theory, 1919–1924," *Slavic and East European Journal*, XII, no. 3 (Fall 1968), 275–96.

33. V, 171.

34. Ev. Zamyatin, "Ia boius'" (1921), *Litsa* (New York: Mezhdunarodnoe Literaturnoe Sodruzhestvo, 1967), pp. 189–90.

35. Anatoly Mariengof, Review of "Pugachev," *Gostinitsa*, 1 (1922).

36. Ibid.

37. Arseny Avraamov, *Voploshchenie-Esenin-Mariengof* (Moscow: Kn-vo "Imazhinisty," 1921).

38. Ryurik Ivnev (pseudonym of M. A. Kovalev), *Chetyre vystrela v Esenina, Kusikova, Mariengofa, Shershenevicha* (Moscow: Kn-vo

"Imazhinisty," 1921), p. 8. See also his "Ob Esenine," in *Sergey Alexandrovich Esenin,* pp. 9–35.

39. Royzman, pp. 4–5. Also published in *Pamiati Esenina.*

40. Ivan Gruzinov, "Pushkin i my," *Gostinitsa,* 1 (1924).

41. Ibid.

42. V. Shershenevich, "Pamiati Sergeya Esenina," *Sovetskoe iskusstvo,* 1 (1926), 52–54.

43. Ryurik Ivnev and others, "Pis'mo v redaktsiiu," *Novyi zritel',* 35 (1924), 16.

44. "Ne peredovitsa," *Gostinitsa,* 1 (1922).

45. See also Nils Ake Nilsson, *The Russian Imaginists,* Stockholm Slavic Studies 5 (Stockholm: Almquist & Wiksell, 1970).

46. See V, 83–84.

47. Ivnev, "Ob Esenine," pp. 11, 15.

48. Roman Arensky (pseudonym of Zinaida Gippius), "Zemlia i kamen'," *Golos zhizni,* 14 (1915), 12–13.

49. See Ivanov-Razumnik, *Rossiia i Inoniia,* pp. 35–59.

50. V, 148–49.

51. V, 153.

52. V, 49. See also his estimate of *Kotik Letaev* as the "most highly gifted work of our time": V, 63 (1918).

53. V, 22.

54. See Blok, Letter to M. P. Murashev, March 9, 1915, VIII, 441.

55. See for instance V, 9; Blok, Diary for January 4, 1918, VII, 313–14; Blok, Letter to S. A. Esenin, April 22, 1915, VIII, 444–45; F. Dolidze, "Vstrechi s Sergeem Eseninym," *Zaria Vostoka,* October 5, 1960, p. 3; M. Babenchikov, "Esenin," in *Sergey Alexandrovich Esenin,* p. 40; Kirillov, p. 175; Livkin, p. 117; and Chernyavsky, p. 148.

56. See Blok, V, 10; 36, 43, 48, 51–53; 68, 71; 92–94; 102–103, 107–108, 117–29.

57. V, 81.

58. V, 82.

59. V. Bryusov, "Kliuchi tain" (1904), in *Ot simvolizma do "Oktiabria,"* pp. 45–47.

60. Valery Bryusov, "Smysl sovremennoi poezii," *Khudozhestvennoe slovo,* 2 (1920), 44–46.

61. V. Bryusov, "Vchera, segodnia i zavtra russkoi poezii," *Pechat' i revoliutsiia,* 7 (1922), 59.

62. V, 17.

63. Gorodetsky, pp. 139–40.

64. V, 17.

65. Chernyavsky, p. 147.

178 SERGEY ESENIN

66. Rozanov, "Moe znakomstvo s Eseninym," p. 33.
67. V, 22.
68. See for instance Mariengof, *Vospominaniia o Esenine*, pp. 9, 13, 15; Izryadnova, p. 101; N. Khomchuk, "Esenin i Klyuev," *Russkaia Literatura*, no. 2 (1958), p. 156; and Georgy Ivanov, *Peterburgskie zimy* (New York: Izd-vo Imeni Chekhova, 1952), pp. 93–95.
69. See Gordon McVay, "Nikolay Klyuev, Some biographical materials," in Nikolay Klyuev, *Sochineniia*, ed. G. P. Struve and B. A. Filippov, 2 vols. (A. Neimanis Buchvertrieb und Verlag, 1969), I, 195–96.
70. See Erlikh, *Pravo na pesn'*, pp. 96–98; and his "Chetyre dnia," pp. 89–97.
71. See Nikolay Klyuev, *Polnoe sobranie sochinenii*, ed. and with an introduction by Boris Filippov, 2 vols. (New York: Izd-vo Imeni Chekhova, 1954). See also Klyuev, *Sochineniia*. In volume two of the latter edition a number of prose pieces written by Klyuev between 1914 and 1919 have been included for the first time. On p. 367 is the only reference to Esenin: Klyuev lists him along with Glinka, Rimsky-Korsakov, Pushkin, Dostoevsky, and Vrubel, who, he implies, were great artists and in whose works the "spirit of eternity and immortality blows."
72. Klyuev, *Polnoe sobranie sochinenii*, II, 85–90.
73. Ibid., pp. 85, 86, 87, 88.
74. Ibid., p. 87.
75. Ibid., pp. 87–90. He also compared Esenin to a shark out for a kill, or an "eager pup." See also Klyuev's poem "V stepi chumatskaya zola," in *Pamiati Esenina*, p. 188, where he compared Esenin to a Judas who had consequently lost his poetic power.
76. Klyuev, *Polnoe sobranie sochinenii*, II, 103–11.
77. Ibid., p. 104
78. Ibid., pp. 103–104.
79. Ibid., pp. 106–107.
80. Ibid., p. 105.
81. Ibid., p. 108.
82. Ibid., p. 111.
83. Klyuev, *Sochineniia*, II, 362.
84. Ibid., p. 367.
85. See *Pamiati Esenina*, p. 189.
86. Viktor Shklovsky, "Zeitgenossen und Synchronisten," in *Die Serapionsbrueder von Petrograd*, trans. and ed. by Gisela Drohla (Frankfurt am Main: Insel Verlag, 1963), pp. 260–71. Translated from the original in *Gamburgskii shchet* (Leningrad, 1928). For a "Serapion" response to Esenin's poetry (generally negative) see Ilya

Notes and References 179

Gruzdev, "Russkaia Poeziia v 1918–23 gg.," *Kniga i revoliutsiia*, 3 (1923), 36–37.

87. Shklovsky, pp. 261, 263, 265, 270.

88. Ibid., pp. 262–64.

89. Yury Tynyanov, "Promezhutok" (1924), in his *Arkhaisty i novatory* (Leningrad: Priboy, 1929), pp. 542–44.

90. Ibid., pp. 544–45.

91. Ibid., pp. 545–46.

92. Ibid., pp. 546–47.

93. For Formalism see B. Aykhenbaum, "V ozhidanii literatury," *Russkii sovremennik*, 1 (1924), 280–90; and Yury Tynyanov, "Literaturnoe segodnia," *Russkii sovremennik*, 1 (1924), 291–306. See also Victor Erlich, *Russian Formalism: History-Doctrine*, 2d. rev. ed. (The Hague: Mouton & Co., 1965), pp. 171–91; Gleb Struve, *Soviet Russian Literature, 1917–50* (Norman: University of Oklahoma Press, 1951), pp. 192–201; and Ewa M. Thomson, *Russian Formalism and Anglo-American New Criticism: A Comparative Study* (The Hague: Mouton & Co., 1971), *passim*.

94. See, for instance, David Burlyuk, and others, "Poshchechina obshchestvennomu vkusu," in *Ot simvolizma do Oktiabria*, pp. 99–100.

95. See, for instance, N. Aseev and others, "Lef. Programma" (1923), in N. L. Brodsky, Lvov-Rogachevsky and N. P. Sidorov, eds., *Literaturnye manifesty: ot simvolizma k Oktyabriu* (Moscow: Federatsiia, 1929), pp. 228–37; and "Soglashenie' Moskovskoi assotsiatsii proletarskikh pisatelei (MAPP) i gruppy 'LEF' " (1923), *Literaturnye manifesty*, pp. 245–47.

96. A. Kruchenykh and V. Khlebnikov, "Slovo kak takovoe: o khudozhestvennykh proizvedeniiakh" (1923), in *Ot simvolizma do Oktiabria*, pp. 106–108.

97. A. Kruchenykh, V. Khlebnikov, and G. Petnikov, "Deklaratsiia zaumnogo yazyka," *Ot simvolizma do Oktiabria*, pp. 153–54.

98. A. Kruchenykh, *Chernaia taina Esenina* (Moscow: By the author, 1926), prod. no. 136, pp. 3–11.

99. Ibid., pp. 12–17. One wonders whether Kruchenykh had read Galant's "O dushevnoi bolezni S. Esenina," an article that pinpointed precisely the same symptoms.

100. Kruchenykh, *Chernaia taina Esenina*, p. 21.

101. See for instance, A. Kruchenykh, *Esenin i Moskva kabatskaia* (Moscow: By the author, 1926), prod. no. 135b, p. 10; A. Kruchenykh, *Gibel' Esenina* (Moscow: By the author, 1926), prod. no. 134b, pp. 6–8, 12–14, 17–18; and A. Kruchenykh, *Liki Esenina ot kheruvima do khuligana (Esenin v zhizni i v portretakh)* (Moscow: By the author, 1926), prod. no. 157, pp. 4, 7, 8, 9–10, 17.

102. A. Kruchenykh, *Novyi Esenin (O pervom tome "Sobraniia stikhotvorenii")* (Moscow: By the author, 1926), prod. no. 138, pp. 5–7.

103. Ibid., pp. 9, 13–14, 17, 20–22.

104. A. Kruchenykh, "Psevdo-krest'ianskaia poeziia: Esenin i ego evangelisty," in V. N. Blumenfeld, V. F. Pletnev, and N. F. Chuzhak, eds., *Na putiakh iskusstva: sbornik statei* (Moscow: "Proletkult," 1926), pp. 157, 164, 159, 165–70, 171–72, 174.

105. A. Kruchenykh, *O stat'e Bukharina protiv Esenina* (Moscow: By the author, 1927), p. 3.

106. Vadim Shershenevich, "Russkii futurizm: osnovy futurizma," in *Ot simvolizma do Oktiabria*, p. 145.

107. Nikolay Aseev, "Izbyanoy oboz," *Pechat' i revoliutsiia*, 8 (1922), 11, 45, 39–40, 43.

108. Ibid., pp. 43-45.

109. Nikolay Aseev, "Sergey Esenin" (1926), in his *Zachem i komu nuzhna poeziia* (Moscow: Sovetskii pisatel, 1961), pp. 183–84, 191.

110. See V. Mayakovsky, *Sobranie sochinenii*, edited by L. Yu. Brik and P. K. Luppol, 4 vols. (Moscow: Goslitizdat, 1936), I, e.g. pp. 92; 117; 120, 125; 178, 196–97. Many other instances could be cited.

111. III, 138.

112. Mayakovsky, II, 328–29, 331, 331–54.

113. Ibid., III, 16, 17–18, 19, 21.

114. Ibid., p. 22. On Futurism, see V. Markov, *The Longer Poems of Velimir Khlebnikov*, University of California Publications in Modern Philology, vol. 62 (Berkeley, 1962); V. Markov, *Manifesty i programmy russkikh futuristov*, Slavische Propilaeen, vol. 27 (Munich: Wilhelm Fink Verlag, 1967); and V. Markov, *Russian Futurism: A History* (Berkeley: University of California Press), 1968.

115. See, for instance, P. Sakulin, "Narodyni zlatotsvet," *Vestnik Evropy*, 5 (1916), 204–207, and his *Die Russische literatur* (Wildpark-Potsdam: Akademische Verlagsgesellschaft Athenaion M.B.H., 1927), pp. 231–32. See also P. N. Medvedev, "Puti i pereput'ia Sergeya Esenina," in N. Klyuev and P. N. Medvedev, *Sergey Esenin* (Leningrad: Priboy, 1927), pp. 27–30, 34–35, 37–38, 42, 44–45.

116. See, for instance, N. Kravtsov, ed., *Fol'klor kak iskusstvo slova* (Moscow, 1966), pp. 5–18; 112–39. See also S. G. Lazutin, "Kravtsov, Nikolay Ivanovich," *Kratkaia literaturnaia entsiklopediia* (Moscow: Sovetskaia Entsiklopediia, 1966), III, 793.

117. N. Kravtsov, "Esenin i narodnoe tvorchestvo," in Yu. Sokolov, ed., *Khudozhestvennyi fol'klor*, IV–V (Moscow: GAKhN, 1929),

pp. 193–203. First delivered as a paper on March 8, 1926, and then published in *Khudozhestvennyi fol'klor*, I (1926), 30–53. The *Kratkaia literaturnaia entsyklopediia* presumably ignores this first publication of the article when it states that Kravtsov started publishing in 1929.

118. Ibid., pp. 193–94.
119. Ibid., p. 194 (see I, 68).
120. Ibid., p. 195 (see I, 201).
121. Ibid. (see III, 154).
122. Ibid., pp. 195–96 (see I, 252–53).
123. Ibid., p 196.
124. Ibid., pp. 196–97 (see II, 27).
125. II, 78.
126. Kravtsov, "Esenin i narodnoe tvorchestvo," pp. 196–98 (see I, 225, and IV, 184, respectively). In the 1961–1962 edition of Esenin's works the last two lines above read "The moon's horse skull / Drips gold of decayed spittle."
127. Ibid., pp. 199–203.
128. Ibid., p. 203.
129. B. V. Neyman, "Istochniki eidologii Esenina," in *Khudozhestvennyi fol'klor*, IV–V, pp. 204–17. First published in *Khudozhestvennyi fol'klor*, II–III (1927), pp. 204–17.
130. Ibid., pp. 204–206.
131. Ibid., pp. 206, 210, 211.
132. Ibid., pp. 206–209.
133. Ibid., pp. 209–10 (see II, 88).
134. Ibid., pp. 212–15.
135. Ibid., p. 214.
136. Ibid., pp. 215–17.

Chapter Ten

1. V, 17.
2. See A. Prozorov, "Pereval," *Literaturnaia entsiklopediia* (Moscow: Izd-vo Kommunisticheskoi Akademii, 1934), VIII, 499–501; see also Gleb Glinka, *Pereval: The Withering of Literary Spontaneity in the USSR* (New York: Research Program on the USSR, 1953), pp. 16, 66, and his collected volume *Na Perevale* (New York: Izd-vo Imeni Chekhova, 1954).
3. See M. Dobrynin, "Voronsky, Alexandr Konstantinovich," *Literaturnaia entsiklopediia* (Moscow: Izd-vo Kommunisticheskoi Akademii, 1929), II, 313–18; see also A. G. Dementev, "Voronsky, Alexander Konstantinovich," *Kratkaia literaturnaia entsiklopediia* (Moscow: Sovetskaia Entsiklopediia, 1962), I, 1046–47.

4. See esp. A. Voronsky, "Iskusstvo, kak poznanie zhizni, i sovremennost'," *Krasnia nov'*, 5 (1923), 347–84.

5. A. Voronsky, "O proletarskom iskusstve i o khudozhestvennoi politike nashei partii," *Krasnaia nov'*, 7 (1923), 257–76.

6. See Robert A. Maguire, *Red Virgin Soil: Soviet Literature in the 1920's*, Studies of the Russian Institute, Columbia University (Princeton: Princeton University Press, 1968), pp. 188–259.

7. A. Voronsky, "Literaturnye otkliki," *Krasnaia nov'*, 2, (1922), pp. 258–75.

8. A. Voronsky, "Literaturnye otkliki," in *Na styke: sbornik statei* (Moscow-Petrograd: Gosizdat, 1923), pp. 15, 19, 21.

9. Ibid., pp. 17–18, 20–22.

10. Ibid., pp. 16, 26, 19, 31–32.

11. A. Voronsky, "Ob otshel'nikakh, bezumtsakh i buntariakh," in *Na styke: sbornik statei*, p. 234.

12. Ibid., pp. 234–35.

13. Ibid., pp. 28–29. Voronsky must have known about the poem in advance of its publication in 1922.

14. A. Voronsky, "Sergey Esenin: literaturnyi portret" (1924), *Literaturno-kriticheskie stat'i* (Moscow: Sovetskii pisatel, 1963), pp. 247–48. For the same view see Vyacheslav Polonsky, the editor of the journals *Pechat' i revoliutsiia* (1921–1929) and *Novyi mir* (1925–1931) in his "Pamiati Esenina," *Novyi mir*, 1 (1926), 156, 160–61.

15. Voronsky, "Sergey Esenin: literaturnyi portret," pp. 245, 250, 271, 255–58.

16. Ibid., pp. 250–52, 268, 257, 254–55, 259, 263–64.

17. Ibid., pp. 260–61, 258–59.

18. Ibid., pp. 269–70, 272–73, 248–49, 260–61, 251, 265, 253.

19. Ibid., pp. 258–59.

20. Ibid., p. 273.

21. A. Voronsky, "Literaturnye zametki," *Prozhektor*, 5 (1925), 26.

22. A Voronsky, "Ob otoshedshem," *Krasnaia nov'*, 1 (1926), 227–30, 233–36.

23. A. Voronsky, "Pamiati o Esenine (iz vospominanii)," p. 208.

24. A. Voronsky, "Tugie dni podkhodiat," *Zhurnalist*, 1 (1926), 18–19.

25. Voronsky, "Pamiati o Esenine (iz vospominanii)," p. 214.

26. Leon Trotsky, *Literature and Revolution*, trans. by Rose Strunsky (Ann Arbor: The University of Michigan Press, 1960), p. 221. First published in 1924.

27. Ibid., p. 218.

28. Ibid., p. 217.

29. Ibid., p. 218.

30. Ibid., pp. 56–58, 91–94.

31. Ibid., pp. 66–69.

32. Ibid., pp. 222–23.

33. L. Trotsky, "Pamiati Sergeya Esenina," *Pravda*, January 19, 1926, p. 3.

34. Ibid.

35. Ibid.

36. See the "Tezisy doklada t. Lelevicha, priniatye na I Moskovskoi Konferentsii Proletarskikh Pisatelei, 16 marta 1923 g.," in *Ot simvolizma k Oktiabru*, pp. 186–89.

37. G. Lelevich, "Nashi literaturnye raznoglasiia," in A. Voronsky and others, *Proletariat i literatura: sbornik statei* (Leningrad: Gosizdat, 1925), p. 83.

38. G. Lelevich, "Partiynaia politika v iskusstve," *Na postu*, 4 (1923), 37.

39. G. Lelevich, "O Sergee Esenine," *Oktiabr'*, 3 (1924), 180–82. The title of the last poem mentioned is actually "Vozvrashchenie na rodinu" ("Coming Back Home"), not as Lelevich has it.

40. G. Lelevich, *Sergey Esenin, ego tvorcheskii put'* (Gomel: "Gomelskii Rabochii," 1926), pp. 3–7, 12–18.

41. Ibid., pp. 43–44, 27–28, 35–37, 39–40. Other Octobrists similarly recognized Esenin's peasant psyche as the distinguishing feature of his writing. They also found a comparable creative shift toward the revolution in 1924. See, for instance, D. Furmanov, "Sergey Esenin" (in "Literaturnye zapisi D. Furmanova," 1925), *Voprosy literatury*, 5 (1957), 205–206; Yu. Libedinsky, "O Esenine, vospominanie," *Na literaturnom postu*, 1 (1926), 33–34; Vladimir Kirshon, "Sergey Esenin" (1926), *Izbrannoe* (Moscow: Goslitizdat, 1958), pp. 484, 496–97; and a critic whose rigorous cultural views gravitated toward those of the Octobrists, V. Polyansky, "Sotsial'nye korni russkoi poezii ot simvolistov do nashikh dnei," in his *Voprosy sovremennoi kritiki* (Moscow-Leningrad: Gosizdat, 1927), pp. 173–74. For Esenin's negative cultural and poetic estimate of proletarian writers generally in 1918, see V, 69–73.

42. See V, 135.

43. Lvov-Rogachevsky, "Novokrest'ianskaia poeziia," *Nash put'*, 5 (1919), 58, 60–61.

44. Lvov-Rogachevsky, *Poeziia novoi Rossii. Poety polei i gorodskikh okrain* (Moscow: T-vo "Knigoizd-vo Pisatelei v Moskve," 1919), pp. 119, 174, 120, 155. Hereinafter cited as *Poeziia novoi Rossii*.

45. Ibid., pp. 82, 84, 89, 90–91.

46. Lvov-Rogachevsky, "Novokrest'ianskaia poeziia," pp. 59, 60–61.

47. Lvov-Rogachevsky, *Poeziia novoi Rossii*, p. 92.

48. Ibid., pp. 55, 59, 57, 64, 92.

49. Lvov-Rogachevsky, *Imazhinizm i ego obrazonostsy: Esenin, Kusikov, Mariengof, Shershenevich* (Revel: Ordnas, 1921), pp. 53, 11, 13–14, 16, 33–34, 39, 41, 44, 40.

50. Ibid., pp. 49, 56, 54.

51. Lvov-Rogachevsky, "Pamiati S. A. Esenina," pp. 2, 5, 10–11, 12, 13, 6, 14–15.

52. V. Aleksandrovsky and others, "Deklaratsiia moskovskikh proletarskikh poetov i pisatelei gruppy Kuznitsa" (1921), in *Ot simvolizma k Oktiabrui*, p. 150. See also I. Filipchenko and others, "Deklaratsiia proletarskikh pisatelei Kuznitsa" (1923), *Ot simvolizma k Oktiabriu*, p. 160.

53. N. Lyashko, "Osnovnye otlichitel'nye priznaki proletarskoi literatury" (1922), *Ot simvolizma k Oktiabriu*, pp. 152–53.

54. Aleksandrovsky and others, pp. 151–52. See also Filipchenko and others, p. 165.

55. Lyashko, pp. 155–56.

56. Georgy Yakubovsky, "Poet velikogo raskola: o lirike Sergeya Esenina," *Oktiabr'*, 1 (1926), 132.

57. G. Yakubovsky, "Iskusstvo i ob'ektivnaia deistvitel'nost'," in Voronsky and others, *Proletariat i literatura: sbornik statei*, pp. 90–93.

58. Yakubovsky, "Poet velikogo raskola: o lirike Sergeya Esenina," pp. 132, 141.

59. Ibid., pp. 141, 135. See also a former member of the Smithy, V. A. Krasilnikov, "Sergey Esenin," *Pechat' i revoliutsiia*, 7 (1925), 115–19, 122–23, 125–27, where he undertook a study of the poetic devices and a lexical analysis of his poetry, in the process also emphasizing the powerful Symbolist and Imaginist influence on his poetic work.

60. See, for instance, Georgy Gorbachev, "Otkrytoe pis'mo redaktoru Zvezdy," in Voronsky and others, *Proletariat i literatura: sbornik statei*, pp. 171, 173, 174.

61. Georgy Gorbachev, *Sovremennaia russkaia literatura* (3rd ed.; Moscow-Leningrad: Priboy, 1931), pp. 10–11, 21, 55–60.

Chapter Eleven

1. See, for example, V. Krasilnikov, "Molodye poety," *Na literaturnom postu*, 7–8 (1926), 37; Boris Lavrenev, "Pamiati Esenina kaznennyi degeneratami," *Krasnaia gazeta*, December 30, 1925, p. 4; G. Deev-Khomyakovsky, "Pravda o Esenine," *Na literaturnom postu*,

4 (1926), 35; Leopold Averbakh, "Pamiati Esenina," *Izvestiia*, December 31, 1925, p. 6; and Mikhail Levidov, "Smert' uchit," *Vecherniaia Moskva*, 2 (1926), 2.

2. Gleb Struve, *Geschichte der Sowjetliteratur* (Munich: Wilhelm Goldmann Verlag, 1963), p. 42.

3. See, for instance, G. Pokrovsky, *Esenin-Eseninshchina-religiia*, 2nd. ed. (Moscow: "Ateist," 1930). First edition 1929.

4. N. A. Semashko, "O samoubiistve," *Vecherniaia Moskva*, January 7, 1926, p. 2.

5. N. Semashko, "Ugrozhaet li nam epidemiia samoubiistv? (po povodu samoubiistva poeta Esenina)," *Izvestiia*, January 22, 1926, p. 5.

6. Nikolay Pogodin, "Pod narkozom," *Komsomol'skaia pravda*, July 6, 1926, p. 1.

7. V. A. Gilyarovsky, in *Vecherniaia Moskva*, January 7, 1926, p. 2.

8. Pokrovsky, p. 63.

9. Quoted from *Pravda* in V. Volpin, *Pamiatka o Sergee Esenine*, *4.X. 1895–28. XII. 1925* (Moscow: "Segodnia," 1926), pp. 46–47. See also V. Pyast, "Pogibshii poet," *Krasnaia gazeta*, December 29, 1925, p. 4.

10. Trotsky, "Pamiati Sergeya Esenina," p. 3.

11. Voronsky, "Ob otoshedshem," pp. 228, 232–33, 235. The reference is to the foal in Esenin's poem "Sorokoust" (1920), which tried but failed to outrun a train.

12. Ibid., p. 235.

13. See I. Nusinov, "Radek, Karl Bernardovich," *Literaturnaia entsiklopediia* (Moscow: Izd-vo Kommunisticheskoi Akademii, 1935), IX, 482–86. See also V. Utechin, *Everyman's Concise Encyclopedia of Russia* (London-New York: J. M. Dent & Sons Ltd., E. P. Dutton & Co. Inc., 1961), p. 447.

14. Karl Radek, "Bezdomnye liudi," *Pravda*, June 16, 1926, p. 2.

15. Karl Radek, "Ne termometr vinovat," *Komsomol'skaia pravda*, June 27, 1926, p. 2.

16. A. V. Lunacharsky, "Sergey Esenin," in *Stat'i o sovetskoi literature* (Moscow: Uchpedgiz, 1958), pp. 438–39.

17. Georgy Yakubovsky, "Lirika i sovremennost'. Kolumby liriki," *Oktiabr'*, 5 (1926), 121, 123.

18. Gorbachev, *Sovremennaia russkaia literatura*, p. 61.

19. Kruchenykh, *Gibel' Esenina (kak Esenin prishel k samoubiistvu)* pp. 9–10, 4.

20. A. Kruchenykh, *Prodelki Esenistov* (Moscow: By the author, 1926), prod. no. 140a, pp. 13–14, 5, 9, 11. This was part IV of his

Na bor'bu s khuliganstvom v literature (Moscow: By the author, 1926), prod. no. 140, published separately. Its other parts did not deal with Esenin. See also A. Kruchenykh, *Khuligan Esenin* (Moscow: By the author, 1926), prod. no. 141, pp. 1–2, 24–26. For examples of the negative reaction of proletarian militants to Esenin and Eseninism, see footnote 1 above.

21. Mayakovsky, III, 328–30.

22. Vladimir Mayakovsky, "Vystuplenie na dispute 'Upadochnoe nastroenie sredi molodezhi (Eseninshchina)'," in his *Polnoe sobranie sochinenii* (Moscow: Goslitizdat, 1959), XII, 312–16.

23. Ibid., pp. 317–20. For a response by Fellow Travelers, see, among others: Boris Pilnyak, "O Sergee Esenine," *Zhurnalist*, 1 (1926), 49; Aleksey Tolstoy, "Nekrolog," in *Krasnaia gazeta*, December 31, 1925, p. 5; Leonid Leonov, "Umer poet," *30 dney*, 1926, pp. 17–19; Petr Oreshin, Review of *Sobranie stikhotvorenii*, vol. 1, by S. Esenin, *Krasnaia nov'*, 5 (1926), 235–37; and Petr Oreshin, "Velikii lirik (k godovshchine smerti Sergeya Esenina)," *Krasnaia nov'*, 1 (1927), 242–44; Sergey Gorodetsky, "Tekushchii moment v poezii," *Sovetskoe iskusstvo*, 2 (1926), 22–34; and Sergey Gorodetsky, "Oktiabr' v khudozhestvennoi literature," *Izvestiia*, November 7, 1926, p. 9: Alexander Oksenov, "O sud'be Esenina" (1926), *IMLI*, F. 32, Op. 3, No. 27, pp. 2–5 (five typed pages signed by the author); finally, Pravdukhin, pp. 175–79, 182, 180.

The Fellow Travelers seemed less preoccupied with the social consequences of Esenin's suicide than with the creative implications of Esenin's poetic fate for themselves and their epoch, and with the psychological causes behind his undoing. They were, therefore, less motivated by political or literary group considerations than by a constructive endeavor (in this they resembled the Marxists) to comprehend and explain Esenin's poetic dilemma and significance.

Chapter Twelve

1. Boris Eichenbaum, "Die Theorie der formalen Methode," in *Aufsaetze zur Theorie und Geschichte der Literatur* (Frankfurt a.M.: Suhrkamp Verlag, 1965), p. 9.

2. Fedor Zhits, "Pochemu my liubim Esenina: etiud," *Krasnaia nov'*, 5 (1926), 222, Zhits' italics; see also p. 217.

3. I. N. Rozanov, *Russkaia lirika: ot poezii bezlichnoi — k ispovedi serdtsa. Istoriko-literaturnye ocherki* (Moscow: Zadruga, 1914), p. 10.

Selected Bibliography

PRIMARY SOURCES

1. In Russian

Radunitsa. Petrograd: Izd-vo M. Aver'ianova, 1916.
Goluben'. Petrograd: Izd-vo "Revoliutsionnyi sotsializm," 1918.
Preobrazhenie. Moscow: Izd-vo Moskovskoi trudovoi arteli khudozhni-kov slova, 1918.
Treriadnitsa. Moscow: Izd-vo "Zlak," 1920.
Izbrannoe. Moscow: GIZ, 1922.
Sobranie stikhov i poem, vol. 1. Petrograd-Moscow-Berlin: Izd-vo Z. I. Grzebina, 1922.
Stikhi skandalista. Berlin: Izd-vo I. T. Blagova, 1923.
Moskva kabatskaia. Leningrad: n.p., 1924.
Persidskie motivy. Moscow: Izd-vo "Sovremennaia Rossiia," 1925.
Rus' sovetskaia. Baku: Izd-vo "Bakinskii rabochii," 1925.
Sobranie stikhotvorenii. Moscow-Leningrad: Gosizdat, 1926–1927. 4 vols.
Stikhotvoreniia. Introd. by K. Zelinsky. Moscow: Goslitizdat, 1955. 2 vols.
Sobranie sochinenii. Moscow: Goslitizdat, 1961–1962. 5 vols.
Sobranie sochinenii. Moscow: "Khudozhestvennaia literatura," 1966–1968. 5 vols.

2. In English
Confessions of a Hooligan. Fifty Poems by Sergei Esenin. Tr. and introd. by Geoffrey Thurley. Cheadle: Carcanet Press, 1973.
An Anthology of Russian Verse. Ed. by Avrahm Yarmolinsky. New York: Doubleday and Company, Inc., 1962. Pp. 192–97.
A Book of Russian Verse. Tr. into English by various hands and ed. by C. M. Bowra. Westport, Conn.: Greenwood Press, 1971. Pp. 121–23.
Modern Russian Poetry. Ed. by Vladimir Markov and Merril Sparks. Indianapolis - Kansas City - New York: Bobbs-Merrill, 1967. Pp. 571–85.
Modern Russian Poetry. Tr. and ed. by Olga Andreyev Carlisle and Rose Styron. New York: The Viking Press, 1972. Pp. 105–12.

The Penguin Book of Russian Verse. Introd. and ed. by Dimitri Obolensky. Harmondsworth: Penguin Books Ltd., 1962. Pp. 391–400.

A Second Book of Russian Verse. Tr. into English by various hands and ed. by C. M. Bowra. Westport, Conn.: Greenwood Press, 1971. Pp. 134–37.

SECONDARY SOURCES

AURAS, CHRISTIANE. *Sergej Esenin: Bilder - und Symbolwelt.* Munich: O. Sagner, 1965. A study of Esenin's characteristic colors and types of imagery and their specific functions in his poetic work, divided into three periods, each with its particular way of seeing or dealing with reality.

BELOUSOV, VLADIMIR. *Sergey Esenin. Literaturnaia khronika* (Moscow: Sovetskaia Rossiia, 1969–1970. 2 vols. A "documentary biography" of Esenin. A very useful source for biographical details and data on publication of Esenin's work during his lifetime. Gives the relevant sources for the information compiled.

DUNCAN, IRMA and McDOUGALL, ALLAN ROSS. *Isadora Duncan's Russian Days and Her Last Years in France.* New York: Covici-Friede, 1929. Contains an intimate and human portrait of Esenin, the man behind the image.

GRAAF, FRANCISCA DE. *Sergej Esenin. A Biographical Sketch.* The Hague - Paris: Mouton & Co., 1966. The standard English work on Esenin's life and works; based on her *Serge Esénine, 1895–1925: Sa vie et son oeuvre.* Leyden: E. J. Brill, 1933.

LAFITTE, SOPHIE. *Serge Essénine: Une Etude.* Paris: Editions Pierre Seghers, 1959. An almost lyrical evocation of Esenin's creative tragedy, of his "nostalgic" muse perishing under the optimistic thrust of bolshevism. The study is followed by a representative selection of poems in French translation.

McVAY, GORDON. *Esenin. A Life.* Ann Arbor: Ardis, 1976. The only thorough study of Esenin's life in English.

MARCHENKO, ALLA. *Poeticheskii mir Esenina.* Moscow: Sovetsky pisatel, 1972. The best study of Esenin's poetics.

MARKOV, VLADIMIR. "Legenda o Esenine." *Grani*, 25 (1955), 139–62. A very interesting article, focusing, among other things, on death as a central motif in Esenin's work and suggesting intriguing creative parallels with Lermontov, Gogol, Bunin, and Rilke.

NILSSON, NILS AKE. *The Russian Imaginists.* Acta Universitatis Stockholmiensis, Stockholm Slavic Studies 5. Stockholm: Almquist &

Wiksell, 1970. A timely study of the Russian Imaginists, containing a few pages on Esenin's relations and creative links with the group.

POGGIOLI, RENATO. *The Poets of Russia: 1890–1930.* Cambridge, Mass.: Harvard University Press, 1960. Section V of Chapter 8 is a sensitive poetic appreciation of Esenin in miniature.

PONOMAREFF, CONSTANTIN V. "Death and Decay: An Analysis of S. A. Esenin's Poetic Form." *Canadian Slavonic Papers,* X (Summer 1968), 180–209. An attempt to trace the many faces of death in Esenin's poetry.

————. "The Image Seekers: An Analysis of Imaginist Poetic Theory, 1919–1924." *Slavic and East European Journal,* VII, no. 3 (Fall 1968), 275–96. A first exploration of the Imaginists, including Esenin, their views of art, and their position as artists in Soviet society.

————. "Woman as Nemesis: Card Symbolism in Hebel, Esenin and Pushkin." *Germano-Slavica,* 6 (Fall 1975), 67–70. A brief comparative venture into literary influence and psychological affinities.

PROKUSHEV, YURY, ed. *Sbornik: Vospominaniia o Sergee Esenine.* Moscow: Moskovskii rabochii, 1965. The first post-Stalin collection of memoirs of Esenin. Contains new or additional material first written or published in the 1950s and 1960s. Draws heavily, sometimes in abbreviated form, on the memoir literature of the 1920s. Should be used as a complementary source of information to the latter.

STRUVE, GLEB. *Russian Literature under Lenin and Stalin, 1917–1953.* Norman: University of Oklahoma Press, 1971. A short section on Esenin (pp. 22–26) gives an objective estimate of the poet.

YUSHIN, PETR. *Sergey Esenin. Ideino-tvorcheskaia evoliutsiia.* Moscow: Izdatel'stvo Moskovskogo universiteta, 1969. A Soviet interpretation. Incorporates his earlier *Poeziia Sergeya Esenina, 1910–1923 godov* (Moscow: Izd-vo Moskovskogo Universiteta, 1966), and completes the study of Esenin's poetic development. Contains a study of Soviet, Yugoslav, and Western criticism on Esenin as well as a bibliography of 1462 items. A valuable contribution.

ZAVALISHIN, VYACHESLAV. *Early Soviet Writers.* New York: Frederick A. Praeger Publishers, 1958. A somewhat idealized treatment of Esenin as a peasant poet (pp. 118–30).

Index

191

194

SERGEY ESENIN

Realism, 102, 142
Red Virgin Soil; see Voronsky
Remizov, Aleksey, 119
Revolutionary Romanticism, 139, 151
Revolution of 1917 (February/-March), 18, 19, 39, 63, 136; (October/November), 19, 24, 39, *44-45*, 63, 75, 76, 102, 103, 111, 112, 140, 141, 152, 165
Riddles of the Russian People (Sadovnikov), 134
Romanticism, 33, 39, 102, 103, 106, 107, *108-109*, 148, 151, 162, 164, 165
Royzman, Matvey, 36, 117
Rozanov, Ivan, 37, 65, 115, 118, 121, 166

Sadi, 78
Sadovnikov, Dmitry, 132
St. Petersburg (Bely), 106
Sakulin, Pavel, 20; 16, 135
Sardanovsky, Nikolay, 16
Scythians, 18, 19, 105, *110-13*, 114, 129
"Scythians, The" (Blok), 111
Semashko, Nikolay, *154-55*
"Serapion Brothers," The, 105, 144
Shagane, 79, 80, 81
Shershenevich, Vadim, 34, 114, 117; 18, 105, 149-50, 166
Shestov, Lev, 88
Shiryaevets, Alexander, 65
Shklovsky, Viktor, *123-24;* 164
Silver Dove, The (Bely), 119
Slavs' Poetic Conceptions of Nature, The (Afanasev), 134
Smithy, The, 105, 151, 157
Sobol', Andrey, 156
Solovev, Vladimir, 111

"Snow Mask, The" (Blok), 71
Sontag, Susan, 165
Startsev, Ivan, *34-35*, 61, 65
Stasov, Vladimir, 134
Struve, Gleb, 154
Suicides; *see* Eseninism
Symbolism (Russian), 20, 21, 102, 103, *104-105*, 107, 108, 112, *118-21*, 129, 137, 147, 148, 149, 151, 152, 162, 164

"Three Meetings" (Solovev), 47
Tikhonov, Nikolay, 65
Titovs (Esenin's maternal grand-parents), 15
"To Esenin" (Mayakovsky), 130
Tolstoy, Alexey, 119
Tolstaya, Sofia, 66, 67, 84
Tolstoy, Leo, 67
"Trans-sense" language; *see* Futurism (Russian)
Trediakovsky, Vasily, 117
Trotsky, Lev (pseudonym of L. D. Bronstein), *144-46*, 157; 106, 158, 164
Tynyanov, Yury, 124; 164
Tyutchev, Fedor, 103, 111, 149
"Twelve, The" (Blok), 105, 111

Ustinov, Georgy, *35-36*, 64
Ustinova, Elizaveta, 67, 68

Vinogradskaya, Sofya, 66
Voronsky, Alexander, 64-65, *136-44*, 157-58; 107, 164, 166

Yakubovsky, Georgy, *150-52;* 108, 159

Zamyatin, Evgeny, *116-17;* 105, 119
Zhits, Fedor, 165